LORD SHIVA - THE ONLY OBJECT OF DESIRE ACCORDING TO THE VEDAS

KARTHICK

NOTION PRESS

NOTION PRESS

India. Singapore. Malaysia.

To

Supreme Lord Shiva, Supreme Goddess Parvathi,

All the devotees of Lord Shiva in the entire universe

CONTENTS

FOREWORD

This is a book that enlightens one about how only Lord Shiva is the Object of Desire according to the Vedas. I have been through many books and scripture-based texts but I found that this book is the most unique among them as it covers the Shruti (Vedas and Upanishads) and Smriti (Puranas and Ithihaasaas). This book contains references from all the authentic scriptures and commentaries. It goes on to educate us and tells us that Lord Shiva is the supreme personality and how only he is the object of desire and should be meditated upon.

The author has put a great effort and provided us with many authentic references and meanings from the scriptures. The author also informs us about the benefits of engaging in Shiva bhakti and how one can get all his desires fulfilled and tasks accomplished by the grace of Lord Shiva.

By Shishir Mohan Nigam

****

All the scriptures including Upanishads, Vedas, Puranas, Ithihaasaas talk about the glories of Mahadeva. Talking about the author (Karthick Sir), he has been giving lectures on the glories of Mahadeva, By watching & getting inspired by those lectures, I purchased this amazing book. Whatever the author claims are backed with dozens of scriptural references. There's not a single claim from the author's side. I (being a lord shiva devotee) am fond of reading the glories of Mahadeva and this book Serves the purpose. This book is a commentary on an octet sung by Sage Vishvaanara. It consists of 8 chapters and each Chapter is a commentary for each verse of the octet.

The moment I started reading the book, I was fascinated by the simple yet powerful language the author used to glorify Mahadeva. As Vedas say 'न इति न इति' (neither this, nor that), Lord Shiva can't be described with mere words, but yes, this book is, at par the best book about the glories of Mahadev.

We can say, My lord doesn't measure His domain, nor does he need to. Others do it for him, as Hari and Brahma once did. I give you the assurance that if you read the book with full devotion, you'll come to a clear conclusion that lord Shiva is the only object of desire according to the Vedas.

I Congratulate Mr. Karthick Sir all the very best for the success of this book. May Lord Shiva & Mother Parvathi bless him and all his devotees.

May no moment pass where we do not remember Mahadeva. May he spare no moment in blessing those who remember him.

By - A trifle Shiva bhakta

NAMAH SHIVAYA

By Prince Tyagi

****

"Athāto brahma jijñāsā", this sentence pretty much explains my journey towards the inspiration to read this book. From an atheist who said "I will not believe in god because I don't see him" to a staunch Shaivite who worships shiva as the saguna brahman, this journey has been wonderful. This book has been an important step to reaching this destination of shiva bhakti and understanding Sanatana Dharma.

It's a commonly known misconception among most of the population in the world, that Hinduism is a polytheistic religion. Hinduism is a monotheistic religion with a polytheistic form of worship. That is, on supreme entity manifesting as many. That one supreme entity who is hailed all over the Chaturdasha vidhyasthanams is Shiva. Hence, Shaivism is synonymous with Hinduism in its complete sense. This book wonderfully expounds this truth through various proofs.

Like an orphan looking for affection, a seeker looks for a path. In an age where Shaivism is on the verge of extinction, a few chosen children of Jagan Mata help in guiding the seekers to the right path. Forever, I will be indebted and grateful to the author for guiding me to the sacred path of Shaivism.

By Shashank Swarup

****

ACKNOWLEDGMENTS

First of all, I would like to thank the Supreme Lord Mahadeva & Mother Para Shakti who have graced me with the spiritual knowledge to write this book. Even if one has to chant "SHIVA SHIVA", that also happens only by the grace of Mahadeva. So, I completely dedicate whatever I have learned in the scriptures and the praises I receive to the feet of Bhagavan Shiva & Bhagavathi Para Shakti.

Secondly, I would like to thank my wife who has been my greatest support in writing books on Lord Shiva. She has always been encouraging and motivating me in my spiritual journey. When I published my first book on Lord Shiva in English - "LORD SHIVA - THE ONLY OBJECT OF DESIRE ACCORDING TO THE VEDAS", I wanted the blessings of Mahadeva since it was the first book ever that I wrote on Lord Shiva. She took the first copy of my book, traveled to many Shiva temples and placed them at the feet of Lord Shiva to receive his blessings. If there is someone whom I would thank the most after my Father Parama Shiva & Mother Para Shakti, it is my wife. Thank you for everything, my dear.

INTRODUCTION

My humble prostrations to the lotus feet of Parama Shiva which is caressed by Para Shakti and which even devatas like Brahma, Hari & Indra are still searching for.

My humble salutations to the devotees of Lord Shiva who are eternally present in the highest spiritual world Maha Kailasha engaging in service to Saamba Shiva.

With the grace of the Supreme Lord Parama Shiva, the Supreme Mother Para Shakti & the devotees of Lord Shiva, I am writing my first book **LORD SHIVA - THE ONLY OBJECT OF DESIRE ACCORDING TO THE VEDAS**.

This book contains a detailed commentary on Abhilaasha Ashtakam, an octet sung by Sage Vishvaanara praising Lord Shiva. The word "abhilASha" in Sanskrit means desire (or) wish.

Every verse of Abhilaasha Asthakam is connected with various aphorisms from the Upanishads. By reading this commentary, one would be able to understand that Lord Shiva is the ultimate essence of all the scriptures (Vedas, Upanishads, Puranas, Upa-Puranas, Smritis, Agamas, Ithihaasaas, etc.) and devotional service to him leads one to liberation.

This octet comes in two places in the Puranas with slight modifications. Below are the references:

1) Shiva Maha Purana ShataRudra Samhita Chapter 13 Verses (42-49)
2) Skanda Maha Purana Kaashi Khanda Chapter 10 Verses (126-133)

CHAPTER 1
Lord Shiva the Supreme Absolute Truth

VERSE 1:

एकम्ब्रह्मैवाद्वितीयं समस्तं सत्यं सत्यं नेह नानास्ति किञ्चित् ।
एको रुद्रो न द्वितीयोऽवतस्थे तस्मादेकं त्वां प्रपद्ये महेशम् ।।

ekaM brahmaivAdvitIyaM samastaM satyaM satyaM neha nAnAsti kinchit |
eko rudro na dvitIyo vatasthe tasmAdekaM tvAM prapadye mahesham ||

The Supreme Reality is ONE without a second. It is true. Indeed multiple supreme realities cannot exist. There is only ONE Rudra. There is none equal to him or greater than him. Hence I seek refuge in you alone, the sole great Lord Maheshvara.

COMMENTARY:

Lord Shiva is described as the Ultimate Supreme Being according to the Vedas, Upanishads, Agamas, Smritis, Puranas, Upa-Puranas, Ithihaasaas, etc. This verse talks about many aphorisms from the Upanishads. Let's go through that one by one.

Brihadaranyaka Upanishad 4.4.19:

मनसा एव आप्तव्यम् अनुद्रष्टव्यम् नेह नानाऽस्ति किं चन
मृत्योः स मृत्युमाप्नोति य इह नानेव पश्यति

manasaivAnudraShTavyaM **neha nAnAasti kinchana**
mRityoH sa mRityumApnoti ya iha nAneva pashyati

Brahman (Lord Shiva) is to be realized through the mind. **There are no multiple Gods, the Supreme Reality is Lord Shiva alone.** One who thinks that there are many Gods keeps taking repeated births and deaths.

The above verse from Brihadaranyaka Upanishad uses the phrase "**neha nAnAasti kinchana**" which means that multiple supreme realities cannot exist. The Supreme Reality can be only one and that is Lord Shiva alone. This is confirmed by Sage Vishvaanara where he uses the same phrase when he glorifies Lord Shiva as the Supreme Reality. Lord Shiva is the ultimate cause of all and the sole object of surrender. One who equates Lord Shiva with other devatas like Hari, Brahma & Indra and engages in worshipping them would keep taking repeated births & deaths.

Lord Shiva's divine qualities and characteristics are described as the only object of meditation in the Vedas, Upanishads & Puranas and not that of Brahma, Hari or Indra who are bound by birth, death, old age, disease, the three modes of material nature (goodness, passion & ignorance), lust, anger, etc.

Let's look at some of the references from the Upanishads & Puranas which explain the divine qualities of Lord Shiva who is the only object of meditation.

Kaivalya Upanishad:

हृत्पुण्डरीकं विरजं विशुद्धं विचिन्त्य मध्ये विशदं विशोकम्
अचिन्त्यमव्यक्तमनन्तरूपं शिवं प्रशान्तममृतं ब्रह्मयोनिम्
तमादिमध्यान्तविहीनमेकं विभुं चिदानन्दमरूपमद्भुतम्

hRitpuNDarIkaM virajaM vishuddhaM vichintya madhye vishadaM vishokam
achintyamavyaktamanantarUpaM shivaM prashAntam amRitaM brahmayonim
tamAdimadhyAntavihInamekaM vibhuM chidAnandamarUpamadbhutam

One should meditate in the lotus of the heart on the personality who is difficult to be contemplated, unmanifest (whose form cannot be seen with material eyes), whose forms are infinite, who is all auspicious, immortal, all-pervading, who is the cause of all (Brahma, Vishnu, Indra, etc.), who has no beginning nor middle nor end, who is one and omnipresent, who is consciousness personified and full of Bliss, who is not bound by a material form and who is wonderful.

उमासहायं परमेश्वरं प्रभुं त्रिलोचनं नीलकण्ठं प्रशान्तम्
ध्यात्वा मुनिर्गच्छति भूतयोनिं समस्तसाक्षिं तमसः परस्तात्

umAsahAyaM parameshvaraM prabhuM trilochanaM nIlakaNThaM prashAntam
dhyAtvA munirgachChati bhUtayoniM samastasAkShiM tamasaH parastAt

Uma's spouse, the one who is eternally present with Uma, Para Shakti, Ambika (umAsahAyam); the supreme Lord (parameshvaraM); who is the Lord of the entire universe (prabhuM); the three-eyed (trilochanaM); the blue-necked lord (nIlakaNThaM); peaceful & benevolent (prashAntam), by meditating on this personality a Sage reaches Him (goes to the highest world Maha Kailasha and doesn't return from there) who is the origin of all beings, the witness of all and who is beyond darkness.

Rig Veda Shiva Sankalpa Suktam 24:

कैलासशिखरे रम्ये शङ्करस्य शिवालये
देवतास्तत्र मोदन्ते तन्मे मनः शिवसङ्कल्पमस्तु

kailAsashikare ramye shankarasya shivAlaye
devatAstatra modhanthe tanme manah shiva sankalpam astu

Mahadeva resides in Maha Kailasha which is his Abode (Maha Kailasha is the Ultimate spiritual abode which is beyond Brahma Loka, Vaikuntha, Goloka, Svarga, etc.). All the devatas Hari, Brahma & Indra are eager and delighted to stay there. Let my mind focus on Lord Shiva.

Rig Veda Shiva Sankalpa Suktam 25:

कैलासशिखराभासा हिमवद्गिरिसंस्थिताः
नीलकण्ठं त्रिनेत्रं च तन्मे मनः शिवसङ्कल्पमस्तु

kailAsashikarA bhAsA himavadgiri samsthitAha
nilakantam trinetram cha tanme manah shiva sankalpam astu

(Some readings in Mahaanyaasam Shiva Sankalpa Suktam says कन्यका: (kanyakAha) instead of samsthitAha)

Mahadeva who is three-eyed and blue-necked resides in Maha Kailasha along with the daughter of the mountains. Let my mind focus on Lord Shiva.

Maha Narayana Upanishad:

ऋतं सत्यं परं ब्रह्म पुरुषं कृष्णपिङ्गळम्
ऊर्ध्वरेतं विरूपाक्षं विश्वरूपाय वै नमो नमः

Ritagum satyaM paraM brahma puruSham kRiShNapiNgalam
Urdhvaretam virUpAkSham vishvarUpAya vai namo namaH

The Supreme Reality is Righteousness personified, Truth personified and who is Uma Maheshvara (Ardhanaarishvara; krshna pingala is a very specific epithet used only for Bhagavan Shiva in the Puranas), Supreme of all, odd-eyed (three-eyed). Salutations to him whose form is the universe.

NOTE: The words **krshnapingala, urdhvareta, virUpAksha, mUjavat, krittivAsA, tryambaka, nIlagrivA, etc.** that appear in the Vedas & Upanishads are very specific epithets used only for Bhagavan Shiva in the Puranas.

Lord Shiva is worshipped by devatas Hari, Brahma, Indra, etc.

Maha Narayana Upanishad:

नमो हिरण्यबाहवे हिरण्यवर्णाय हिरण्यरूपाय हिरण्यपतये
अम्बिकापतय उमापतये पशुपतये नमोनमः

namo hiraNyabAhave hiraNyavarNAya hiraNyarUpAya hiraNyapataye
ambikApataya umApataye pashupataye namo namaH

Salutations again and again to Hiranyabahu (whose hands are golden; one who has golden ornaments worn on his arms), Hiranyavarna (whose complexion is golden), Hiranyarupa (He whose form is shining in golden splendor), Hiranyapati (the Lord of riches & all kinds of prosperity), Ambikapati (the consort of Ambika, the Mother of the entire universe), Umapati (The consort and the Lord of Uma), Pashupati (the Lord of all individual souls including Hari, Brahma, Indra, etc.).

Krishna Yajur Veda Taittiriya Samhita 1.8.6, Shukla Yajur Veda Vaajasaneyi Samhita 3.60-61:

त्र्यम्बकं यजामहे सुगन्धिं पुष्टिवर्धनम् । उर्वारुकमिव बन्धनान्मृत्योर्मुक्षीय माऽमृतात्
एषते रुद्र भाग स्तञ्जुषस्व तेनावसेन परो मूजवतोऽती ह्यवतत धन्वा पिनाकहस्तः कृत्तिवासाः

tryambakam yajAmahe sugandhim pushtivardhanam urvArukam iva bandhanAn mrtyor mukshIya mA mrtAt
eshate rudra bhAgastam jushasva tenAvasena paro mUjavatotI havyavatata dhanvA pinAkahastah krittivAsAh

I make a sacrificial offering to Tryambaka (three-eyed Lord Shiva) who has a sweet fragrance, who provides prosperity, health & wealth to the fullest to his dear devotees. Just like a ripe cucumber gets separated from the binding stalk, may I be liberated from death and get immortality (MOKSHA means liberation). Please accept this sacrificial offering, O Rudra who is present in the mountain Mujavat with the Pinaka bow in your hand and wearing the skin of Narasimha as your garment (Lord Shiva wore the skin of Narasimha as his garment after destroying his arrogance).

These are very specific epithets used only for Lord Shiva in the Puranas, Upa-Puranas & Ithihaasaas and not for devatas like Brahma, Vishnu & Indra. There are many more references from the Upanishads & Puranas that can be spoken of. This is just a sample.

Suta Samhita Canto 1 Chapter 2 Verses 19-24:

एवं कृत्वा व्रतं देवा अथर्वशिरसि स्थितम् ।
शान्ता दान्ता विरक्ताश्च त्यक्त्वा कर्माणि सुव्रताः॥
वालाग्रमात्रं विश्वेशं जातवेदस्वरूपिणम् ।
हृत्पद्मकर्णिकामध्ये ध्यात्वा वेदविदां वराः ॥
सर्वज्ञं सर्वकर्तारं समस्ताधारमद्भुतम् ।
प्रणवेनैव मन्त्रेण पूजयामासुरीश्वरम् ॥
अथ तेषां प्रसादार्थं पशूनां पातिरीश्वरः ।
उमार्धविग्रहः श्रीमान्सोमार्धकृतशेखरः ॥
नीलकण्ठो निराधारो निर्मलो निरुपप्लवः ।
ब्रह्माविष्णुमहेशानैरुपास्यः परमेश्वरः ॥
सांनिध्यमकरोद्रुद्रः साक्षात्संसारनाशकः ।
यं प्रपश्यन्ति वेदान्तैः स्वरूपं सर्वसाक्षिणम्

evam krtvA vratam devA atharvashirasi sthitam
shAnta dAntA viraktAscha tyaktvA karmANi suvratAhA

vAlAgramAtram vishvesham jAtavedasvarUpiNam
hrtpadmakarNika madhye dhyAtvA vedavidAm varAhA

sarvajnyam sarvakartAram samasthAdhAram adbhutam
praNavenaiva mantreNa pUjayAmAsurIshvaram

atha teshAm prasAdArtham pashUnAm patir Ishvaraha
umArdhavirgrahah shrImAn somArdhakrtashekharaha

nIlakaNto nirAdhAro nirmalo nirupallavaha
brahmavishnumaheshAnair upAsya parameshvaraha

sannidhyam akarod rudrah sakshAt samsAra nAshakaha
yam prapashyanti vedAntaih svarUpam sarvasAkshiNam

The above reference from Suta Samhita Canto 1 Chapter 2 talks about a supporting fact (Upa Brihmanam) for Atharvashiras Upanishad where all the devatas Hari, Brahma & Indra embellish their body with the holy ashes, wear the Rudraksha garland, chant holy hymns and worship Lord Shiva within their hearts whose divine features alone are to be meditated upon: **The one who is sharing half of his body with Mother Uma, whose throat is blue, who has a moon on his forehead, who is without impurities, who is the Lord of all the Pashus (Pashus are the individual souls which includes everything starting from the blade of grass till Vishnu), true witness, all knowledgeable, highest Ishvara, the cause of all causes including Brahma, Vishnu & Kaala Rudra and who releases the individual soul (Jeevaatmaa) from the repeated cycles of birth and death**.

This supporting fact stated in the Suta Samhita relates to what is told in the **Atharvashiras Upanishad** by the devatas to Lord Shiva:

हृदि त्वमसि यो नित्यं तिस्रो मात्राः परस्तु सः ।

hRidi tvamasi yo nityaM tisro mAtrAH parastu saH

O eternal God Shiva, you are dwelling in the heart of all. You transcend the three states of consciousness (The form to be meditated in the heart is that of Bhagavan Shiva as described in the Suta Samhita which provides the supporting fact for Atharvashiras Upanishad).

वालाग्रमात्रं हृदयस्य मध्ये विश्वं देवं जातरूपं वरेण्यम् ।
तमात्मस्थं येनु पश्यन्ति धीरास्तेषां शान्तिर्भवति नेतरेषाम् ।

vAlAgramAtraM hRidayasya madhye vishvaM devaM jAtarUpaM vareNyam
tamAtmasthaM yenu pashyanti dhIrAsteShAM shAntirbhavati netareShAm

To the wise men who realize **the Supreme God Shiva in the center of the heart who is the Supreme Atman, who is as minute as the end of the hair, omniscient, Lord of the universe who has everything under his control and the best and all**, will attain the eternal peace and not others.

One should understand that Kaala Rudra and Parameshvara are different. Brahma, Narayana & Rudra are created by Parameshvara to do the task of creation, maintenance and destruction. Lord Shiva alone is described as the doer of five activities (creation, maintenance, destruction, concealment & liberation) in the scriptures. The difference between Kaala Rudra and Parameshvara is told everywhere in the Upanishads, Puranas, Upa-Puranas, Ithihaasaas, etc. A reference is given below from Padma Purana.

Padma Purana Paataala Khanda 108th Chapter (How to prepare Sacred Ash) Verses 3,5,6:

य एकः शाश्वतो देवो ब्रह्मवंद्यः सदाशिवः
त्रिलोचनो गुणाधारो गुणातीतोऽक्षरोव्ययः

ya ekah shAshvato devo brahmavandhyah sadAshivaha
trilochano guNAdhAro guNAtIta akshara avyayaha

The eternal God Sadashiva, who is even saluted by devatas like Brahma, Hari & Indra, who has three eyes, who is the support of all virtues, who is SHUDDHA SATTVA (beyond the three modes of material nature: goodness, passion and ignorance), who is not bound by change and who is imperishable.

दक्षिणांगेसृजत्पुत्रं ब्रह्माणं वामतो हरिम्
पृष्ठदेशे महेशानं त्रीन्पुत्रानसृजद्विभुः

dakshiNAnge srujat putram brahmANam vAmato harim
prushTadeshe maheshAnam trInputrAn srujad vibhuhu

He created Brahma from his right limb and Hari from his left limb. He created Mahesha (Kaala Rudra) from his back. In this way, Sadashiva had three sons.

The only thing is that Kaala Rudra has the partial spark of Lord Shiva since he is a partial manifestation of Lord Shiva. He does the task of destruction and merges back into Parama Shiva whereas Brahma, Hari & Indra are individual souls who keep changing and whose positions are attainable by austerities.

Suta Samhita Canto 1 Chapter 2 Verse 34, 35:

अहमेव परं तत्त्वं मत्तो जातं जगत्सुराः ॥

मय्येव संस्थितं नष्टं मत्समो नाधिकः सदा ।
मत्स्वरूपपरिज्ञानादेव संसारनिर्हृतिः ॥

ahameva param tattvam matto jAtam jagat surAhA
mayyeva samsthitam nashTam matsamo nAdhikah sadA
matsvarUpa parijnyAnAdeva samsAra nirhvatihi

Bhagavan Shiva along with Para Shakti appeared in front of the devatas Brahma, Hari & Indra after they had intensely prayed to him. He said to them as follows: "**I alone am the Ultimate Reality, I am the cause of the entire universe, there is nothing equal to or greater than me, only by knowing and meditating on my divine spiritual form, one will get rid of the repeated cycles of birth and death and there is no other way.**"

As the Vedas say **temevam vidvAn amrita iha bhavathi nAnyah panthA ayanAya vidyathe** which means knowing the Supreme Lord Shiva, thus in this life itself, one transcends the repeated cycles of birth and death and reaches the eternal world Maha Kailasha. There is no other path that can lead one to liberation. The same is told in the **Shvetashvatara Upanishad 3.8**.

These are the qualities and characteristics of Lord Shiva that one should focus on in meditation and not that of the devatas like Brahma, Hari (including Hari's incarnations like Narasimha, Rama, Krishna, etc.) & Indra. Since they themselves are bound to destruction, they cannot lead an individual soul to immortality. Only by the grace of the immortal Lord Shiva, the individual souls can attain immortality. The word "**amrita**" (**immortality**) appears in the Upanishads many times referring to Lord Shiva alone.

Jabala Upanishad:

अथ हैनं ब्रह्मचारिण ऊचुः किं जप्येनामृतत्वं ब्रूहीति ॥
स होवाच याज्ञवल्क्यः । शतरुद्रियेणेत्येतान्येव ह वा अमृतस्य नामानि ॥
एतैर्ह वा अमृतो भवतीति एवमेवैतद्याज्ञवल्क्यः ॥

atha hainaM brahmachAriNa UchuH kim japyenAmRitatvaM brUhIti
sa hovAcha yAjnyavalkyaH shatarudriyeNetyetAnyeva ha vA amRitasya nAmAni
etairha vA amRito bhavatIti evamevaitadyAjnyavalkyaH

The students addressed their Guru who is Sage Yajnavalkya: "Please tell us by what holy recitation one attains **immortality**"? Sage Yajnavalkya replied: "By chanting **Shatarudriya** (**RUDRAM that comes in the center of the Vedas**). These are the names of the **immortal one Parama Shiva**. Reciting these names, one verily attains **immortality**."

Rig Veda 10.90.2 & Shvetashvatara Upanishad 3.15:

पुरुष एवेदꣳ सर्वं यद् भूतं यच्च भव्यम् ।
उतामृतत्वस्येशानो यदन्नेनातिरोहति ॥

puruSha evedagum sarvaM yad bhUtaM yachcha bhavyam |
utAmRitatvasyeshAno yadannenAtirohati ||

The Veda Purusha (Supreme Being) Parama Shiva alone is that which is, that which was and that which is yet to be. He is the **Lord of Immortality** and of whatever that grows by food.

Atharvashiras Upanishad:

यो वै रुद्रः स भगवान्यच्चामृतं तस्मै वै नमोनमः

yo vai rudraH sa bhagavAnyachcha amRitaM tasmai vai namonamaH

He who is Rudra is verily the Supreme Lord (**bhagavAn**). My salutations to Rudra who is the personification of immortality.

If one has to achieve that immortal state in this life itself then one has to worship that personality who is ageless, birthless and that is Mahadeva alone.

Matsya Purana Chapter 154 Verses 180, 181:

ब्रह्मविष्णिवन्द्रमुनयो जन्ममृत्युजरार्दिताः।
तस्यैते परमेशस्य सर्वे क्रीड़नका गिरे! ।।

आस्ते ब्रह्मा तदिच्छातः संभूतो भुवनप्रभुः।
विष्णुर्युगे युगे जातो नानाजातिर्महातनुः ।।

brahma vishNu indra munayo janma mrtyu jarAditAhA
tasyaite parameshasya sarve krIdanakA gire

Aste brahmA tadichAtah sambhUto bhuvana prabhuhu
vishNur yuge yuge jAto nAnAjAtir mahAtanuhu

Sage Narada says to Himavaan: "Brahma, Vishnu & Indra are bound by birth, old age, disease and death. They are instruments in the hands of Parameshvara. It is through the wish of Mahadeva that Brahma and Vishnu are the Lords of their respective domains (Brahma Loka & Vaikuntha)."

Pancha Brahma Upanishad Verse 13:

अवस्थात्रितयातीतं तुरीयं ब्रह्मसंज्ञितम् ब्रह्मविष्ण्वादिभिः सेव्यं सर्वेषां जनकं परम्

avasthAtritayAtItam turIyaM brahmasamjnitam brahma viShNvAdibhiH sevyam sarveShAm janakaM param

Tatpurusha is above the three states of consciousness (vaishnvAnara, taijasa, prAgnya), he is the fourth (Turiya), existence, consciousness and bliss personified. He is the Supreme father of Brahma and Vishnu and is worshipped by them.

Rig Veda 9.96.5, Sama Veda Puurvaarchikaa Chapter 5 Sloka 527, Sama Veda Uttaraarchikaa Chapter 5 Sloka 943:

सोमः पवते जनिता मतीनां जनिता दिवो जनिता पर्थिव्याः |
जनिताग्नेर्जनिता सूर्यस्य जनितेन्द्रस्य जनितोत विष्णोः ||

somah pavate janitA matInAm janita divo janitA prithivyAhA
janitAgner janitA sUryasya janitendrasya janitota vishNOh

Para Shakti & Parama Shiva (Shiva + Uma → SOMA, RUDRAM 8th Anuvaaka: namah somAya cha) glorified by holy hymns who begot Earth, Heaven, Agni, Surya, Indra & Vishnu.

The same is present in the **Bhasma Jabala Upanishad** where Parama Shiva proclaims that he along with Para Shakti creates all of them including Hari, Brahma, Surya, Indra, etc.

These are some sample references. There are many more references showcasing the Jeevatvam of Brahma, Hari & Indra whose positions can be attained by sAdhanA (austerities).

A true devotee of Bhagavan Shiva is not interested in attaining the positions of Hari, Brahma & Indra. He/She would consider the positions of Hari, Brahma & Indra to be equal to the dust at their feet as they are temporary.

He/She would always be interested in serving the lotus feet of Parama Shiva, Para Shakti and devotees of Bhagavan Shiva and go back to the world of Maha Kailasha which is the highest, eternal & indestructible, from where there is no return.

Garuda Purana Canto 1 Chapter 23 Verses 54-57:

बद्धपद्मासनासीनः सितः षोडशवार्षिकः ।।
पञ्चवक्त्रः कराग्रैः स्वैर्दशभिश्चैव धारयन् ।
अभयं प्रसादं शक्तिं शूलं खट्वाङ्गमीश्वरः ।।
दक्षैः करैर्वामकैश्च भुजंगं चाक्षसूत्रकम् ।
डमरुकं नीलोत्पलं बीजपूरकमुत्तमम् ।।
इच्छाज्ञानक्रियाशक्तिस्त्रिनेत्रो हि सदाशिवः ।
एवं शिवार्च्चनध्यानी सर्वदा कालवर्जितः ।।

baddhapadmAsanAsInaH sitaH ShoDashavArShikaH |
panchavaktraH karAgraiH svairdashabhishchaiva dhArayan |
abhayaM prasAdaM shaktiM shUlaM khaTvANgamIshvaraH |
dakShaiH karairvAmakaishcha bhujaNgaM chAkShasUtrakam |
damarukaM nIlotpalaM bIjapUrakamuttamam |
ichChAjnAnakriyAshaktistrinetro hi sadAshivaH |
evaM shivArchanadhyAnI sarvadA kAlavarjitaH |

Lord Shiva should be meditated upon as white in color, sixteen years old seated in Padmaasana, having five faces, ten hands, five on the right carry Abhaya, Prasaada, Shakti, Shula, Khatvaanga and the left ones carry serpent, Akshasutra, drums, blue lotus, pomegranate. SadaShiva is three-eyed. He has Iccha Shakti (power of desire), Kriya Shakti (power of action) and Jnaana Shakti (power of knowledge). A person who worships Lord Shiva like this will become deathless.

Yoga Tattva Upanishad Verses 99-101, Yoga Yajna Valkya Smriti Chapter 8 Verses 22-24:

बिन्दुरूपं महादेवं व्योमाकारं सदाशिवम्
शुद्धस्फटिकसङ्काशं धृतबालेन्दुमौलिनम्
पञ्चवक्त्रयुतं सौम्यं दशबाहुं त्रिलोचनम्
सर्वायुधैर्धृताकारं सर्वभूषणभूषितम्
उमार्धदेहं वरदं सर्वकारणकारणम्

bindurUpaM mahAdevam vyomAkAram sadAshivam
shuddhasphaTikasaNkAsham dhRitabAlendumaulinam
panchavaktrayutam saumyam dashabAhum trilochanam
sarvAyudhairdhRitAkAram sarvabhUShaNabhUShitam
umArdhadeham varadam sarvakAraNakAraNam

One should contemplate on SadaShiva Mahadeva who is in the form of Bindu, who is shining like pure crystal, who has the crescent moon on his forehead, five-faced, ten hands, three eyes, who has a beautiful countenance, armed with all weapons, adorned with all ornaments, having Para Shakti Uma on one half of his body and ready to grant favors and who is the cause of all causes.

Meditation on Lord Shiva is regarded as the greatest of all according to the Vedas. Lord Shiva is meditated upon by even devatas like Brahma, Hari & Indra for salvation. There are some misconceptions raised by ignorant people saying that Lord Shiva meditates on someone, but Lord Shiva doesn't meditate on anybody as he is the overlord of everything. Lord Shiva himself says that in many places.

Padma Purana Paataala Khanda Chapter 114 (Dialogue between Lord Shiva and Rama) Verses 247, 248 (The same is present in Narada Purana Purva Bhaga Chapter 79 Verses 200, 201):

शंकर उवाच-
ध्याये न किंचिद्गोविंद न नमस्येह किंचन
नोपास्ये कंचन हरे न जपिष्येह किंचन

किंतु नास्तिकजंतूनां प्रवृत्त्यर्थमिदं मया
दर्शनीयं हरे ते स्युरन्यथा पापकारिणः

shankara uvAcha
dhyAye na kinchid govinda nana masyeha kinchana

nopAsye kanchana hare na japishye ha kinchana

kintu nAsti kanchtUnAm pravrtyarthamidam mayA
darshanIyam hare tesyur anyathA pApakAriNaha

Shankara says to Brahma, Vishnu & Indra: **I am not meditating upon anyone. I am not saluting anyone. I am not waiting upon anyone. I shall not mutter any prayer invoking anyone**, but I have to exhibit this for leading the unbelievers to activity. Otherwise, they will be sinners.

The same thing has been mentioned in many other places in the scriptures. So the words of the ignorant who try to denigrate Lord Shiva should be discarded as it is just told out of their hatred towards Lord Shiva.

The meditation on Saamba Shiva is the highest of all as his form alone is spiritual and beyond all the three modes of material nature. The forms of Brahma, Hari, Indra & Lakshmi are material and bound to destruction.

Lord Shiva can be meditated in different ways. Ardhanaarishvara, Chidambara Nataraajaa, Thiruvaarur Thyaagaraajaa, Kalyaana Sundara Murthy, Uma Maheshvara, Somaa Skanda Murthy, Mahaa Sadaashiva Murthy (25-faced), SadaaShiva Murthy (5-faced, 10-handed), Chandrakshekara Murthy, Baala Shiva, Tripura Samhaara Murthy, Sharabheshvara, etc. These meditations are widely mentioned in the Vedas, Upanishads, Agamas, Puranas, Upa-Puranas & Ithihaasaas.

Rig Veda Shiva Sankalpa Suktam 18:

परात् परतरो ब्रह्मा तत्परात् परतो हरिः
तत्परात् परतोऽधीशस्तन्मे मनः शिवसङ्कल्पमस्तु

parAt parataro brahmA tatparAt parato hariH
tatparAt parato dhIshastanme manaH shivasaNkalpamastu

The greatest of the greatest is Brahma, but greater than him is Hari, but greater than Brahma & Hari is Shiva, Mahadeva, Shambhu, Ishana, Ishvara. Let my mind focus on Shiva alone and not anyone else.

Only by surrendering, engaging in unflinching devotion, hearing about Lord Shiva and focusing on the divine form of Maheshvara and Para Shakti together, one can transcend the repeated cycles of birth and death. One can never transcend the ocean of worldly existence by surrendering to Hari, Brahma or Indra. Another point to be noted is that, the Supreme Reality has a form. He is not formless as described by the Maayaavaadis. He is described as formless sometimes in the scriptures but that doesn't mean he doesn't have a form. His **spiritual divine form** cannot be seen with material eyes. His form is beyond all the material forms and indestructible. Sometimes to describe Mahadeva's omnipresence, Upanishads describe him as formless. The Shiva Linga represents his all-pervasiveness. He appeared as an infinite column of fire (**AGNI STHAMBA**) to crush the EGO of Brahma & Hari. But he has a divine spiritual form that should be contemplated upon within the Linga. "**That form cannot be seen with material eyes**" is stated in many aphorisms in the Upanishads.

Shvetashvatara 4.20, Pancha Brahma 19, Mahanarayana 1.11, Katha 2.3.9 Upanishads:

न सन्दृशे तिष्ठति रूपमस्य

na sandRishe tiShThati rUpamasya

This means that Lord Shiva's divine spiritual form cannot be seen with our material eyes. Only by intense devotion and also by the blessings of the GURU, one can have the vision of Lord Shiva and go back to Maha Kailasha to serve him eternally, after which one doesn't take birth.

Mahadeva appears as an infinite pillar (Agni Sthamba) to destroy the EGO of Brahma & Hari

ekamevAdvitIyam - Chandogya 6.2.1, 6.2.2

Sage Vishvaanara uses this ekamevAdvitiyam in his song of praise to Lord Shiva which means the Supreme Reality is one without a second. We shall see some references for this in the Upanishads and Puranas.

Atharvashiras Upanishad:

एको रुद्रो न द्वितीयाय तस्मै य इमांल्लोकानीशत ईशनीभिः
प्रत्यङ्जनास्तिष्ठति संचुकोचान्तकाले संसृज्य विश्वा भुवनानि गोप्ता

eko rudro na dvitIyAya tasmai ya imAmllokAnIshata IshanIbhiH
pratyaNjanAstiShThati samchukochAntakAle saMsRijya vishvA bhuvanAni goptA

Shvetashvatara Upanishad 3.2:

एकोहि रुद्रो न द्वितीयाय तस्थुर्य इमाँल्लोकानीशत ईशनीभिः
प्रत्यङ् जनास्तिष्ठति सञ्चुकोचान्तकाले संसृज्य विश्वा भुवनानि गोपाः

eko hi rudro na dvitIyAya tasthur ya imAmllokAnIshata IshanIbhiH
pratyaNjanAstiShThati samchukochAntakAle saMsRijya vishvA bhuvanAni gopAH

Rudra is truly one; for the knowers of Brahman do not admit the existence of a second (there is no one equal to greater than him); He alone rules all the worlds by His powers. He dwells as the inner Self of every living being. After having created all the worlds, He, their protector, takes them back into Himself at the end of time.

Krishna Yajur Veda Taittiriya Samhita 1.8.6:

पशूनागं् शर्मासि शर्म यजमानस्य शर्म मे यच्छैक **एव रुद्रो न द्वितीयाय**

pashUnAgum sharmAsi sharma yajamAnasya sharma me yacchaika **eva rudro na dvitIyAya**

Lord Shiva is described as the ultimate protector; the protector of the sacrifices and rituals and he is the protector of all individual souls. Lord Shiva is described as one without a second. There is nothing that is equal or greater than him.

(This verse is recited as a part of Mahaanyaasam which is recited before chanting the Shata Rudriyam)

The epithet **eko rudro na dvitIyAya** comes 3 times in the Vedas & Upanishads & many times in the Puranas indicating the supremacy of Lord Shiva. The Upanishads Atharvashiras, Shvetashvatara, etc. glorify Mahadeva alone. We have 30 supporting facts (Upa Brihmanams) for Atharvashiras Upanishad showcasing that it glorifies Lord Shiva and it was sung by Brahma, Vishnu & Indra to Lord

Shiva and not anyone else. One has to understand whom the Vedas & Upanishads are glorifying by depending on the Smritis. The Shruti (Vedas) can never be understood without the help of Smriti (Puranas, Ithihaasaas). The Puranas give various references to showcase that Atharvashiras is an Upanishad that glorifies Lord Shiva. Suta Samhita Canto 1 Chapter 2 provides a detailed story of Atharvashiras Upanishad as seen before and there are many references in other Puranas highlighting the essence of this Upanishad as Lord Shiva. As you can see the same verse "**eko rudro na dvitIyAya**" in Atharvashiras Upanishad comes in Shvetashvatara Upanishad too. Shvetashvatara Upanishad is given by Sage Shvetashvatara who is described as a great devotee of Lord Shiva in the Puranas (Shiva, Kurma, Saura, etc.). Also in Suta Samhita Yajna Vaibhava Khanda Brahma Gita Chapter 11, Sage Suta talks about the supporting fact describing Shvetashvatara Upanishad as glorifying Lord Shiva alone.

Sage Shvetashvatara is described as practicing Atyaashrama or Paashupata vow which means adorning one's body with the holy ashes, wearing the Tripundra (holy ashes on the forehead) & wearing the garland of Rudraksha, hearing stories related to Shiva, singing songs praising Shiva (Shiva Naama Sankeertanam), worshipping the Shiva Linga and Shiva Vigraha (divine form) and meditating on Shiva along with the mother Para Shakti in one's heart. This is how Atyaashrama or Paashupata or Shaambhava or Shiro Vratam is described in the Puranas.

This also shows that the Paashupata vow mentioned in the Atharavashiras Upanishad and Atyaashrama vow mentioned in the Shvetashvatara & Kaivalya Upanishads go hand in hand as the Puranas say that both Atyaashrama and Paashupata mean one and the same.

Saura Purana 27.28:

yat tat pAshupatam yogam antyAshramam iti shrutam
guhyam tat sarva vedeshu vedavidbhir anushtitham

Whatever is described as **Paashupata** in the Vedas (Shruti) is same as **Atyaashrama** (Both are synonymous). It is the secret of the secrets present in the Vedas and the vow is practiced by people who are experts in the Vedas.

Kaarana Agama Chapter 1 Verse 9: Parama Shiva says to Para Shakti:

अत्याश्रमं पाशुपतं शाम्भवं तच्छिरोव्रतम्
इत्येवं नामभिः पुण्यैर्निगमान्तेषु गीयते ॥

atyAshramam pAshupatam shAmbhavam tacchirovratam
ityevam nAmabih punyair nigamAntheshu gIyathe

In Upanishads, Shiro Vratam is appreciated by sacred names such as Atyaashrama, Paashupata and Shaambhava.

All these four names are synonymous and they refer to Bhasma Dhaaranam, Tripundra Dhaaranam, Rudraaksha Dhaaranam, hearing the praises of Lord Shiva, singing the names of Lord Shiva, meditating on the divine form of Lord Shiva, etc. These 4 names are repeatedly mentioned in the Upanishads. They do not talk about Urdhva Pundra, as Urdhva Pundra is Avaidika (not mentioned anywhere in the authentic Upanishads). Within the Sri Vaishnava tradition, there are 2 Urdhva Pundras. Totally, there are 7 kinds of Urdhva Pundras (Sri Vaishnava Tenkalai, Sri Vaishnava Vadakalai, Madhva, Gaudiya, Swami Narayan, Vallabha & Nimbarka). How can all the 7 kinds of Urdhva Pundras be authentic and they apply those respective Urdhva Pundra to Vishnu. But there are many references in the scriptures where Vishnu is described with Tripundra, Bhasma, and Rudraksha in the Upanishads & Puranas (one reference is given below). Urdhva Pundra is not in conformity with the Vedas. Even Tapta Mudra → imprinting the Shankha and Chakra on the shoulders is not in conformity with the Vedas. Bhasma Dhaaranam, Tripundra Dhaaranam, Rudraksha Dhaaranam alone is **Vaidikam (in alignment**

with the Vedas). This verily talks about how Shaivism alone is in complete conformity with the Vedas & Upanishads. All other religions like Buddhism, Jainism, Shaktam, Kaumaram, Vaishnavam, Sauram, Ganapatyam & Maayaavaadam lead you to Shaivism after many births.

When one applies the Bhasma on their body one should always have the realization that starting from the blade of grass till Vishnu - all are bound to destruction (bound to become ashes one day). Lord Shiva alone is the Supreme Reality and he is the only object of meditation, worship & surrender.

Nowadays, ignorant people out of hatred towards Lord Shiva, try to attribute these Upanishads to other devatas. They are fools of the first order. Their EGO is not ready to accept the Supremacy of Lord Shiva which is spoken of everywhere in the Vedas, Upanishads & Puranas. We see Daksha Prajaapati was egoistic and ignorant about Lord Shiva and finally his EGO was crushed by Virabhadra (a devotee of Lord Shiva who appeared from the hair locket of Mahadeva). Mahadeva is the destroyer of EGO of all the demons and also devatas like Brahma, Vishnu & Indra.

The Upanishads & Puranas do talk about Brahma & Vishnu adorning the holy ashes and praying to Lord Shiva eternally for attaining liberation (Moksha). Here is a verse showcasing Vishnu with the sacred ash:

Brihat Jabala 6th Brahmana 7th Verse (The same is present with a slight modification in Padma Purana Paataala Khanda Chapter 105 The Importance of Sacred Ash Verse 223):

ततोभस्म भक्षयेति हरिमाह हरस्ततः
भक्षयिष्येशिवं भस्म स्नात्वाहं भस्मना पुरा

tato bhasma bhakShayeti harimAha harastataH
bhakShayiShye shivaM bhasma snAtvAhaM bhasmanA purA

Vishnu says to Lord Shiva: I shall eat the sacred ash. Formerly I have bathed with the sacred ash.

Bathing with the sacred ash (Bhasma) and eating the sacred ash is done by Vishnu to get the knowledge of Lord Shiva. We hesitate to apply Bhasma on our forehead and body but here Vishnu bathes with the sacred ash and eats the sacred ash like food to get the knowledge of Lord Shiva. From this we should definitely understand how sacred ash is very important to attain Lord Shiva. After seeing the divine form of Lord Shiva within his heart, Vishnu falls at the feet of Lord Shiva and says:

Brihat Jabala 6th Brahmana 10th Verse, Padma Purana Paataala Khanda Chapter 105 Verse 234: Vishnu says to Lord Shiva:

न शक्यं भस्मनोज्ञानं प्रभावं तेकुतोविभो
नमस्तेऽस्तुनमस्तेऽस्तुत्वामहं शरणं गतः

na shakyaM bhasmano jnAnaM prabhAvam te kuto vibho
namastestu namastestu tvAmaham sharaNam gataH

I don't have the capability to understand the power of the sacred ash; when can I ever understand your glories, O Mahadeva? Salutations to you, salutations to you. I seek your refuge.

Like this, there are many references where Brahma, Vishnu & incarnations of Vishnu, Indra, Lakshmi, Sarasvathi & Indrani are always with holy ashes and engage in worshipping Lord Shiva and Para Shakti.

Skanda Maha Purana Kaashi Khanda Uttaraardha Chapter 87 Verse 85: Rudra is one without a second (एको रुद्रो न द्वितीयः → eko rudro na dvitIyaha).

Shiva Maha Purana VaayavIya Samhita Section 1 Chapter 3 Verse 8, 9:

जीवैरेभिरिमांल्लोकान्सर्वानीशो य ईशते
य एको भागवान् रुद्रो न द्वितीयोऽस्ति कश्चन

सदा जनानां हृदये संनिविष्टो ऽपि यः परैः
अलक्ष्यो लक्षयन्विश्वमधितिष्ठति सर्वदा

jIvair abhirimAllokAn sarvAn Isho ya Ishate
ya eko bhagavAn rudro na dvitIyosti kaschana

sadA janAnAm hrudaye sannivishtopi yah paraih
alakshyo lakshayan vishvam adhitishTati sarvadA

Lord Shiva rules all the worlds through the individual souls (Jeevaatmaas). There is none second to him. Though he has entered and is ever present in the hearts of the people, he is invisible to others; he views and controls the universe always.

Shiva Maha Purana VaayavIya Samhita Section 2 Chapter 6 Verse 13:

अंबिकापतिरीशानः पिनाकी वृषवाहनः
एको रुद्रः परं ब्रह्म पुरुषः कृष्णपिंगलः

ambikApatir ishAnah pinAki vrshavAhanaha
eko rudrah param brahma purushah krshna pingalaha

That Supreme Reality is described as the husband of Ambika, one without a second, dark and tawny (Ardhanaarishvara, Uma Maheshvara).

Skanda Maha Purana Kaashi Khanda Uttaraardha Chapter 95 Verse 56:

एको रुद्रो न द्वितीयो यतस्तद्ब्रह्मैवैकं नेह नानास्ति किंचित्
यद्यप्यन्यः कोपि वा कुत्रचिद्वा व्याचष्टां तद्यस्य शक्तिर्मदग्रे

eko rudro na dvithIyo yathasthad brahmaivaikam neha nAnAsthi kinchith
yadyapyanyaha kopivA kutrachidvA vyAchashtAnthadyasya shaktir madhagre

Sage Vyasa says to Lord Shiva: Brahman alone is one. There cannot be multiple supreme realities. Hence Rudra is the only one. There is none second to him. If there be anyone else anywhere, let him who has the capacity to say so, explain it to me.

So the import of the first verse is that Sage Vishvaanara glorifies Lord Shiva to be one without a second; there is none equal to or greater than him. He applies the aphorisms from the Vedas & Upanishads to Lord Shiva. Since Lord Shiva alone is the Supreme Reality, he surrenders unto him alone. Human life is said to be precious because humans are given the sixth sense compared to the five senses given to animals. The sixth sense should be utilized in how to attain the Supreme Reality Lord Shiva. One should not waste the precious human life by worshipping devatas like Brahma, Hari, Indra or Lakshmi by which we would again be entangled in taking repeated births and deaths. As Atharvashikha Upanishad says **shiva eko dhyeyaha (Shiva is the only object of meditation)**, caste aside everybody and worship Lord Shiva who alone is the giver of material desires & emancipation from the repeated cycles of birth and death.

CHAPTER 2
Lord Shiva the cause of all causes

VERSE 2:

एकः कर्ता त्वं हि सर्वस्य शम्भो नानारूपेष्वेकरूपोस्य रूपः ।
यद्वत्प्रत्यप्स्वर्क एकोप्यनेकस्तस्मान्नान्यं त्वां विनेशं प्रपद्ये ।।

ekaH kartA tvaM hi sarvasya shaMbho nAnArUpeShvekarUposya rUpaH |
yadvatpratyapsvarka ekopyanekastasmAn nAnyaM tvAM vineshaM prapadye ||

There is only one creator and you are the sole creator of everything. You have one ultimate form and you appear in many different forms, just as the sun appears as many in different waters and you are beyond all material forms. Hence I do not resort to anyone except you.

COMMENTARY:

Mahadeva alone is described as the cause of all causes in the Vedas, Upanishads, Puranas & Ithihaasaas. He is the cause of even devatas like Brahma, Hari & Indra. Let us look at some references.

Harivamsha Purana 2-74-34: Krishna says to Parama Shiva:

अहं ब्रह्मा कपिलो योऽप्यनन्तः पुत्राः सर्वे ब्रह्मणश्चातिवीराः ।
त्वत्तः सर्वे देवदेव प्रसूता एवं सर्वेशः कारणात्मा त्वमीड्य ।।

ahaM brahmA kapilo yopyanantaH putrAH sarve brahmaNashchAtivIrAH
tvattaH sarve devadeva prasUtA evaM sarveshaH kAraNAtmA tvamIDyaH

O the lord of lords Parama Shiva. Myself, Brahma, Kapila Muni, Sesha and all the valiant sons of Brahma who conquered their internal enemies - **all are**

created from you. Hence you are the lord of all. Hence you are the only one worthy of praise who is the lord of all.

Here Krishna includes himself along with Brahma, Adi Sesha & all the sages describing Parama Shiva as being the ultimate cause of all.

This is in line with what is told in **Mahabharata Drona Parva Chapter 201 Verses 95, 96** by Sage Vyasa to Ashvattama:

स एष रुद्र भक्तश्च केशवो रुद्रसम्भवः
कृष्ण एव हि यष्टव्यो यज्ञैश्चैव सनातनः
सर्वभूतभवं ज्ञात्वा लिङ्गमर्चति यः प्रभोः

sa esha rudra bhaktashcha keshavo rudra sambhavaha
krushNa eva hi yashtavyo yajnyaishchaiva sanAtanaha
sarvabhUtabhavam jnyAtvA lingam archati yah prabhoh

Keshava is the devoted worshipper of Rudra who originated from Rudra himself. Keshava always worships the Shiva Linga, regarding Lord Shiva to be the origin of the entire universe & all individual souls.

Harivamsha Purana 2-74-32: Krishna says to Para Shakti & Parama Shiva:

यल्लिङ्गाङ्कं यच्च लोके भगाङ्कं सर्वं सोम त्वं स्थावरं जङ्गमं च ।
प्राहुर्विप्रास्त्वां गुणिनं तत्त्वविज्ञास्तथा ध्येयामम्बिकां लोकधात्रीम् ।।

yalliNgANkaM yachcha loke bhagANkaM sarvaM soma tvaM sthAvaraM jaNgamaM cha
prAhurviprAstvAM guNinaM tattvavijnA stathA dhyeyAmambikAM lokadhAtrIm

O the great lord accompanied with Mother Uma. The fixed and movable entities of this world marked by masculine and feminine genders, are the manifestations of both of you. The learned ones, knowledgeable about the principles, call you the one with divine qualities and worship Ambika as the mother of the world.

Pancha Brahma Upanishad Verses 18 & 19:

आदावन्ते च मध्ये च भाससे नान्यहेतुना
मायया मोहिताः शम्भोर्महादेवं जगद्गुरुम्

न जानन्ति सुराः सर्वे सर्वकारणकारणम्
न सन्दृशे तिष्ठति रूपमस्य परात्परं पुरुषं विश्वधाम

AdAvante cha madhye cha bhAsase nAnyahetunA
mAyayA mohitAH shambhormahAdevam jagadgurum

na jAnanti surAH sarve **sarvakAraNakAraNam**
na sandRishe tiShThati rUpamasya parAtparaM puruSham vishvadhAma

He shines in himself in the past, present and future depending on none else (Everybody including Brahma, Vishnu, Indra & Lakshmi are dependent on him). All the devatas like Brahma, Vishnu & Indra do not realize him, bewildered by the Maya Shakti of Shambhu, Mahadeva, the Guru of the universe and the **cause of all the causes**. His spiritual divine form cannot be seen by material eyes. He is the **highest of the highest**, the support of the universe, the Supreme person from whom the universe manifests.

Mundaka Upanishad 3.1.3:

यदा पश्यः पश्यतेरुक्मवर्णं कर्तारमीशं पुरुषं ब्रह्मयोनिम्
तदा विद्वान् पुण्यपापेविधूय निरञ्जनः परमं साम्यमुपैति

yadA pashyaH pashyate rukmavarNaM **kartAramIshaM** puruShaM brahmayonim
tadA vidvAn puNyapApe vidhUya niranjanaH paramaM sAmyamupaiti

When the seer beholds the **golden personality, Creator of the Creators and the cause of all causes Lord Shiva, the Supreme Lord**, the Purusha, the progenitor of Brahma, then the wise seer shakes off merit and demerit, becomes spotless and attains the Saarupya (attains the form of Lord Shiva) → (One point to be noted here is even after the individual soul attains the form of Lord Shiva it still is subservient to Lord Shiva and remains the eternal servant of Parama Shiva & Para Shakti in Maha Kailasha).

Shvetashvatara Upanishad 3.9, Maha Narayana 12.13:

यस्मात् परं नापरमस्ति किञ्चिद्यस्मान्नणीयोन ज्यायोऽस्ति कश्चित्
वृक्ष इव स्तब्धोदिवि तिष्ठत्येकस्तेनेदं पूर्णं पुरुषेण सर्वम्

yasmAt paraM nAparamasti kinchidyasmAnnaNIyo na jyAyosti kashchit
vRikSha iva stabdho divi tiShThatyekastenedaM pUrNaM puruSheNa sarvam

The whole universe is filled by the Veda Purusha (Veda Purusha is Parama Shiva, Upanishads say: **puruSho vai rudraH**), to whom **there is nothing superior**, from whom there is nothing different, than whom there is nothing either smaller or greater; who stands alone, motionless as a tree, established in His own glory.

Shvetashvatara Upanishad 6.9:

न तस्य कश्चित् पतिरस्ति लोके न चेशिता नैव च तस्य लिङ्गम्
स कारणं करणाधिपाधिपो न चास्य कश्चिज्जनिता न चाधिपः

na tasya kashchit patirasti loke na cheshitA naiva cha tasya liNgam
sa kAraNaM karaNAdhipAdhipo na chAsya kashchijjanitA na chAdhipaH

Bhagavan Shiva has no master in this world, no ruler, nor is there even a sign of Him by which He can be inferred. He is **the ultimate cause of all** and the ruler of individual souls. **He is without a progenitor or controller**.

Atharvashikha Upanishad 3:

कारणं कारणानां ध्याता कारणं तुध्येयः सर्वैश्वर्यसम्पन्नः शंभुराकाशमध्ये

kAraNam kAraNAnAm dhyAtA kAraNam tu dhyeyaH sarvaishvaryasampannaH shaMbhurAkAshamadhye

The cause of all the causes is not the meditator. The cause alone is to be meditated upon. Shambhu who is the Lord of all, and the one endowed with all the perfections, is to be meditated in the middle of the ether (of the heart).

शिव एको ध्येयः शिवंकरः सर्वमन्यत्परित्यज्य समस्ताथर्वशिखैतामधीत्य

shiva eko dhyeyaH shivamkaraH sarvamanyatparityajya samastAtharvashikhaitAmadhItya

Bhagavan Shiva alone is to be meditated upon, Shiva the Giver of good. Give up all else including devatas like Brahma, Vishnu & Indra. Thus, concludes the Atharvashikha.

Yoga Tattva Upanishad Verses 98-101 & Yoga Yajna Valkya Smriti Chapter 8 Verses 22-25:

बिन्दुरूपं महादेवं व्योमाकारं सदाशिवम्
शुद्धस्फटिकसङ्काशं धृतबालेन्दुमौलिनम्
पञ्चवक्त्रयुतं सौम्यं दशबाहुं त्रिलोचनम्
सर्वायुधैर्धृताकारं सर्वभूषणभूषितम्
उमार्धदेहं वरदं **सर्वकारणकारणम्**

bindurUpaM mahAdevam vyomAkAram sadAshivam
shuddhasphaTikasaNkAsham dhRitabAlendumaulinam
panchavaktrayutam saumyam dashabAhum trilochanam
sarvAyudhairdhRitAkAram sarvabhUShaNabhUShitam

umArdhadeham varadam **sarvakAraNakAraNam**

One should contemplate on SadaShiva Mahadeva who is in the form of Bindu, who is shining like pure crystal, who has the crescent moon on his forehead, five faces, ten hands, three eyes, who has a beautiful countenance, armed with all weapons, adorned with all ornaments, having Para Shakti Uma on one half of his body and ready to grant favors and the cause of all causes.

In the Skanda Maha Purana Kaashi Khanda Uttaraardha Chapter 95 Sage Vyasa enters Kaashi and says that Vishnu is the Supreme out of EGO (ahankAra) and all the sages were stunned to hear such a say from the mouth of Vyasa. Nandi (the bull carrier of Lord Shiva) by his mere sight paralyzes the arms of Vyasa. At that time Vishnu comes there and he says as follows:

Skanda Maha Purana Kaashi Khanda Uttaraardha Chapter 95 Verses 48-52:

ततो गुप्तं समागम्य विष्णुर्व्यासमभाषत
अपराद्धं महच्चात्र भवता व्यास निश्चितम्

तवैतदपराधेन भीतिर्मेपि महत्तरा
एक एव हि विश्वेशो द्वितीयो नास्ति कश्चन

तत्प्रसादादहं चक्री लक्ष्मीशस्तत्प्रभावत
त्रैलोक्यरक्षासामर्थ्यं दत्तं तेनैव शंभुना

तद्भक्त्या परमैश्वर्यं मया लब्धं वरात्ततः
इदानीं स्तुहि तं शंभुं यदि मे शुभमिच्छसि

अन्यदापि न वै कार्या भवता शेमुषीदृशी
पाराशर्य इति श्रुत्वा संज्ञया व्याजहार ह

tato guptam samAgamya vishNur vyAsama bhAshata
aparAddham mahachAtra bhavatA vyAsa nischitam

tavaitadaparAdhena bhItirmepi mahatharA
eka eva hi vishvesho dvitIyo nAsti kaschana

tatprasAdAdaham chakrI lakshmIshastat prabhAvata
trailokya rakshAsAmarthyam datham tenaiva shambhunA

tad bhaktyA param aishvaryam mayA labdham varAthataha
idAnIm stuhi tam shambhum yadi me shubham ichasi

anyad api na vai kAryA bhavatA shemusHidrushI
pArAsharya iti shrutvA samjnyayA vyAjahAra ha

Vishnu spoke to Sage Vyasa: "O Vyasa, a great offense has certainly been committed by you. Even I am greatly afraid due to this offense of yours. There is only one Lord of the universe and he is Vishvesha (Lord Shiva). There is no one else. I am the discus-bearer, due to his favor. I am the Lord of Lakshmi due to his power. It was by Shambhu himself that the capacity to sustain the three worlds was granted to me. Due to my devotion to him, the greatest prosperity (aishvarya) that I possess was obtained as a boon from him. If you desire my welfare, eulogize Shambhu alone. Do not entertain a thought like this to eulogize me on any other occasion O son of Paraashara."

After which Sage Vyasa sings a beautiful octet for Lord Shiva glorifying him to be the Supreme Reality and none else.

Skanda Maha Purana Kaashi Khanda Uttaraardha Chapter 95 Verse 56:

एको रुद्रो न द्वितीयो यतस्तद्ब्रह्मैवैकं नेह नानास्ति किंचित्
यद्यप्यन्यः कोपि वा कुत्रचिद्वा व्याचष्टां तद्यस्य शक्तिर्मदग्रे

eko rudro na dvithIyo yathasthad brahmaivaikam neha nAnAsthi kinchith
yadyapyanyaha kopivA kutrachidvA vyAchashtAnthadyasya shaktir madhagre

Sage Vyasa says to Lord Shiva: Brahman alone is one. There cannot be multiple supreme realities. Rudra is the only one. There is none second to him. If there is anyone else anywhere, let him who has the capacity to do so, explain it to me.

Sage Vyasa ends the octet by saying (Verse 63):

नान्यं देवं वेद्म्यहं श्रीमहेशान्नान्यं देवं स्तौमि शंभोर्ऋतेऽहम्
नान्यं देवं वा नमामि त्रिनेत्रात्सत्यं सत्यं सत्यमेतन्मृषा न

nAnyam devam vedhmyaham shrI maheshA nAnyam devam sthoumi shambho rtheham
nAnyam devam vA namAmi trinetrAth sathyam sathyamethanmrushA na

I do not know any other Lord than Sri Mahesha; I do not eulogize another Lord except Shambhu; I do not bow down to a Lord other than the Three-eyed One. This is the truth, the truth, the truth, not a lie.

Kurma Purana Canto 2 (Ishvara Gita) Chapter 3 Verses 20, 21:

नास्ति मत्तः परं भूतं मां विज्ञाय मुच्यते
नित्यं हि नास्ति जगति भूतं स्थावरजङ्गमम्
ऋते मामेकमव्यक्तं व्योमरूपं महेश्वरम्

nAsti mathah param bhUtam mAm vijnyAya muchyate
nityam hi nAsti jagati bhUtam sthAvara jangamam
rte mAm ekam avyaktam vyomarUpam maheshvaram

Lord Shiva says: **There is none greater than me, the ultimate cause. By realizing me alone one is liberated.** The living beings including the mobile and immobile ones in the universe are not eternal with the exception of me, Maheshvara.

There are many more references like this from different Puranas where all of them finally surrender to Lord Shiva including the devatas like Brahma, Vishnu & Indra. Lord Shiva alone is the cause of all causes who should be meditated upon for achieving liberation and not anyone else.

Sage Vishvaanara says that Lord Shiva has one ultimate form and he also appears in many other forms.

Mahadeva is said to have one ultimate form (Mula Murti) in Maha Kailasha which is the highest spiritual world. Parama Shiva & Para Shakti are served there, by crores and crores of liberated individual souls.

The most spoken form of Lord Shiva in the Vedas, Upanishads, Agamas, Puranas, etc. is the form where he is described as crystal white in color, with five heads (Sadyojaataa, Vaamadeva, Aghora, Tatpurusha, Ishaana), ten hands, three eyes, who has a pleasing countenance, adorned with all ornaments, with Bhasma all over his body, having Para Shakti (or) Uma (or) Ambika (or) Lalitha Tripurasundari sitting on his left lap.

This five-headed, ten-handed form of Lord Shiva is the essence of the Bhagavad Gita. Nowadays people think that Bhagavad Gita is the word of Krishna and it is a Vaishnaite scripture. But one who analyzes all the scriptures in detail will definitely come to the understanding that Bhagavad Gita is the words of Lord Shiva and it is preaching Shiva Tattva. Krishna (or) Vishnu is just an instrument who comes to convey the message of Lord Shiva to Arjuna. Let's see some interesting references in the scriptures to understand how the essence of the Bhagavad Gita is Lord Shiva.

Kurma Purana Canto 1 Chapter 30 Verses 60-62:

दृष्टवानसि तं देवं विश्वाक्षं विश्वतोमुखम् ।
प्रत्यक्षमेव सर्वेशं रुद्रं सर्वजगन्मयम् ।।

ज्ञानं तदैश्वरं दिव्यं यथावद् विदितं त्वया ।
स्वयमेव हृषीकेशः प्रीत्योवाच सनातनः ।।

गच्छ गच्छ स्वकं स्थानं न शोकं कर्त्तुमर्हसि ।
व्रजस्व परया भक्त्या शरण्यं शरणं शिवम् ।।

drushtavAnasi tam devam vishvAksham vishvatomukham
pratyaksham eva sarveshAm rudram sarva jaganmayam

jnyAnam tad aishvaram divyam yathAvad viditam tvayA
svayameva hrushIkeshah prItyovAcha sanAtanaha

gacHa gacHa svakam sthAnam na shokam kartum arhasi
vrajasva parayA bhaktyA sharaNyam sharaNam shivam

Sage Vyasa says to Arjuna: You have directly perceived Lord Shiva who has universal vision, who has faces all around who is the very embodiment of the universe. That divine lordly knowledge about Lord Shiva has been precisely understood by you. Vishnu himself came as GURU and recounted it to you. Do go to your own abode. It does not behoove you to grieve. With the greatest devotion seek refuge in Lord Shiva the only personality who is worthy of being the refuge.

Similar to what Sage Vyasa says to Arjuna, Mahadeva's universal form is also explained in the Upanishads.

Shvetashvatara Upanishad 3.3, Maha Narayana Upanishad, Shiva Sankalpa:

विश्वतश्चक्षुरुत विश्वतोमुखो विश्वतोबाहुरुत विश्वतस्पात् ।
सं बाहुभ्यां धमति सम्पतत्रैर्द्यावाभूमी जनयन् देव एकः ॥

vishvatashchakShuruta vishvatomukho vishvatobAhuruta vishvataspAt |
saM bAhubhyAM dhamati sampatatrair dyAvAbhUmI janayan deva ekaH ||

Lord Shiva's eyes are everywhere, faces everywhere, arms everywhere and feet everywhere. He brings together all the beings with his arms, encompasses them with his feet, having produced heaven and earth and he still remains as one without a second.

Also, there are many other references stating Bhagavad Gita was originally given by Lord Shiva. The second Canto of Kurma Purana talks about Ishvara Gita the knowledge given by Lord Shiva. At the end of the Ishvara Gita, it describes how this knowledge was passed on from one sage to another sage. One verse goes on to say:

Kurma Purana Canto 2 (Ishvara Gita) Chapter 11 Verses 131, 132:

नारायणोऽपि भगवान् देवकीतनयो हरिः
अर्जुनाय स्वयं साक्षात् दत्तवानिदमुत्तमम्

nArAyaNopi bhagavAn devakitanayo harihi
arjunAya svayam sAkshAt dattavAn idam uttamam

Narayana, Hari, the son of Devaki gave this excellent knowledge about Lord Shiva to Arjuna.

All these references confirm the fact that it is Lord Shiva who actually showed the universal form (vishvarUpa) in Bhagavad Gita and not Krishna. Krishna comes as Guru for Arjuna to explain about Pashupati Shiva Tattva. Also, the Ishvara Gita that was originally given by Lord Shiva was passed on as Bhagavad Gita as stated in the above reference from Kurma Purana.

Mahabharata Ashwamedha Parva Chapter 16 Verses 6-7:

यत्तु तद्भवता प्रोक्तं पुरा केशव सौहृदात्
तत्सर्वं पुरुषव्याघ्र नष्टं मे व्यग्रचेतसः

मम कौतूहलं त्वस्ति तेष्वर्थेषु पुनः पुनः

yattu tadbhavatA proktam purA keshava sauhrudAt
tat sarvam purusH vyAgra nastam me vyagra chetasaha
mama kautUhalam tvasti teshvartheshu punah punaha

Arjuna asks Krishna: Whatever you said to me on the battlefield Keshava has all been forgotten by me in consequence of the fickleness of my mind. Repeatedly, however, I have been curious to know the subject of those truths.

Krishna replies to Arjuna (Verses 10-13):

न च साऽद्य पुनर्भूयः स्मृतिर्मे सम्भविष्यति
नूनमश्रद्दधानोऽसि दुर्मेधा ह्यसि पाण्डव

न च शक्यं पुनर्वक्तुमशेषेण धनंजय
स हि धर्मः सुपर्याप्तो ब्रह्मणः पदवेदने

न शक्यं तन्मया भूयस्तथा वक्तुमशेषतः
परं हि ब्रह्म कथितं योगयुक्तेन तन्मया

na cha sAdhya punarbhUyah smruthirme sambhavishyati
nUnamashraddhadhAnosi durmedhA hyasi pANdava

na cha shakyam punarvaktum ashesHeNa dhananjaya
sa hi dharmah suparyApto brahmaNah padavedane

na shakyam tanmayA bhUyastathA vaktum ashesHataha
param hi brahma kathitam yogayuktena tanmayA

The recollection of all that I told you on the battlefield will not come to me now. Without a doubt, O son of Pandu, you are destitute of faith and you're understanding is not good. **It is impossible for me, O Dhananjaya to repeat**

everything in detail that I said on that occasion. That religion about which was discoursed to you then is more than sufficient for understanding Brahman (Supreme Reality Parama Shiva). **I cannot discourse on it again in detail. I discoursed to you on the Supreme Brahman, having concentrated in Yoga.**

Krishna expresses his inability to provide the same discourse that he gave to Arjuna on the battlefield as he was in Yogic Union with Parama Shiva (**param hi brahma kathitam yoga yuktena tan mayA**) when Bhagavad Gita was recited. Supporting this fact, Bhagavad Gita 11.8 says दिव्यं ददामि ते चक्षु: पश्य मे **योगमैश्वरम्** (divyam dadAmi te cakshuh pashya me **yogam aishvaram**) which means "**O Arjuna, with divine eyes, look at the ultimate form of Ishvara (Lord Shiva)**". Here the word "**yoga**" is used as before. It explains how Krishna was in Yogic Union with Ishvara (Parama Shiva). The references from Kurma Purana also attest to the fact that it was Lord Shiva who showed the universal form to Arjuna.

Mahabharata Drona Parva Chapter 202 Verses 4-11:

अर्जुन उवाच ।
सङ्ग्रामे न्यहनं शत्रूञ्शरौघैर्विमलैरहम् ।
अग्रतो लक्षये यान्तं पुरुषं पावकप्रभम् ।।

ज्वलन्तं शूलमुद्यम्य यां दिशं प्रतिपद्यते ।
तस्यां दिशि विदीर्यन्ते शत्रवो मे महामुने ।।

तेन भग्नानरीन्सर्वान्मद्भग्नान्मन्यते जनः ।
तेन भग्नानि सैन्यानि पृष्ठतोऽनुव्रजाम्यहम् ।।

भगवंस्तन्ममाचक्ष्व को वै स पुरुषोत्तमः ।
शूलपाणिर्मया दृष्टस्तेजसा सूर्यसन्निभः ।।

न पद्भ्यां स्पृशते भूमिं न च शूलं विमुञ्चति ।
शूलाच्छूलसहस्राणि निष्पेतुस्तस्य तेजसा ।।

arjuna uvAcha
samgrAme nyahanam shatrUn sharaughair vimalair aham
agrato lakshaye yAntam purusHam pAvakaprabham

jvalantam shUlamudhyamya yAm disham pratipadhyate
tasyAm dishi vidIryante shatravo me mahAmune

tena bhagnAnarIn sarvAn madbhagnAn manyate janaha
tena bhagnAni sainyAni prushTatonuvrajAmyaham

bhagavams tanmamAchakshva ko vai sa purusHothamaha
shUlapANir mayA drushtastejasA sUryasannibhaha

na padbhyAm sprushate bhUmim na cha shUlam vimuchati
shUlAn shUla shasrANi nisHpetustasya tejasA

Arjuna asked Sage Vyasa: O great Sage, while I was engaged in slaying my foes in battle with showers of bright shafts, I continually beheld before me, proceeding in front of my chariot, a person of blazing splendor and endued with the effulgence of fire. Wherever he proceeded with his uplifted lance, all the hostile warriors were seen to be killed before him. Killed in reality by him, people regarded the foes to have been killed by me. I only destroyed those who were already destroyed by him. O holy one, tell me who was that foremost of persons, armed with lance, resembling the sun himself in energy, that was thus seen by me? He neither touched the earth with his feet nor did he hurl his lance even once. In consequence of his infinite energy, thousands of lances were issued out of that one lance held by him and killed all the warriors.

व्यास उवाच ।
प्रजापतीनां प्रथमं तैजसं पुरुषं प्रभुम् ।
भुवनं भूर्भुवं देवं तेजसां प्रवरं प्रभुम् ।।

ईशानं वरदं पार्थ दृष्टवानसि शङ्करम् ।

तं गच्छ शरणं देवं वरदं भुवनेश्वरम् ।।

महादेवं महात्मानमीशानं जटिलं विभुम् ।
त्र्यक्षं महाभुजं रुद्रं शिखिनं चीरवाससम् ।।

vyAsa uvAcha
prajApatInAm prathamam taijasam purusHam prabhum
bhuvanam bhUrbhuvam devam tejasAm pravaram prabhum

IshAnam varadam pArtha drushtavAnasi shankaram
tam gaccha sharaNam devam varadam bhuvaneshvaram

mahAdevam mahAtmAnam IshAnam jatilam vibhum
tyaksham mahAbhujam rudram shikhinam chIravAsasam

Sage Vyasa replied Arjuna: O Arjuna, you have seen none other than Lord Shiva, the first cause from whom have sprung the Prajapatis, that puissant Being endued with great energy, he is the embodiment of heaven, earth & sky, the Divine Lord, the protector of the universe, the great Master, the giver of boons, also the ultimate ruler (Ishana). Surrender to that boon-giving Deity who is the lord of the universe. He is called Mahadeva, Supreme Soul, the one and only Lord who is with matted locks on his head, the abode of auspiciousness. He has three eyes and mighty arms, he is called Rudra (remover of all sorrows), with his locks tied in the shape of a crown and his body is covered with animal skins.

The above reference in Mahabharata is when Arjuna after the fifteenth day of the Mahabharata war goes to Sage Vyasa and poses the question, who was the personality that was helping him on the battlefield killing all his enemies and he gets the reply that it was Lord Shiva who had killed all his enemies on the battlefield and Arjuna was just used as an instrument. It was only by the grace of Lord Shiva that Krishna & Pandavas were able to win the war and not otherwise. This is beautifully connected with the below Bhagavad Gita verse.

Bhagavad Gita 11.32:

कालोऽस्मि लोकक्षयकृत्प्रवृद्धो लोकान्समाहर्तुमिह प्रवृत्त: ।
ऋतेऽपि त्वां न भविष्यन्ति सर्वे येऽवस्थिता: प्रत्यनीकेषु योधा: ॥

kAlosmi lokakshayakrt pravruddho lokAn samAhartum iha pravruttah
rtepi tvAm na bhavishyanti sarve yevasthitAh pratyanIkeshu yodhAh

Time, I am, the great destroyer of all the worlds and I have come here to destroy all people. With the exception of you the Pandavas, all the soldiers here on both sides will be slain.

Now we can relate this to the reference in the last chapter of Drona Parva as stated before this. It is Bhagavan Shiva who destroyed the enemies of the Pandavas in the Mahabharata war and not Krishna or Arjuna. It is Bhagavan Shiva who conveys the message of the Bhagavad Gita using Krishna as an instrument. Bhagavan Shiva alone is the essence and the sole object of surrender according to the Bhagavad Gita.

UNIVERSAL FORM OF LORD SHIVA

There is another interesting reference in Padma Purana where Vishnu explains to Lakshmi that Saamba Shiva is the essence of Bhagavad Gita and Lord Shiva's form is verily the form of Bhagavad Gita.

Padma Purana Uttara Khanda Chapter 175 Verse 5, 7-13:

शयालुरसि दुग्धाब्धौ भगवन्केन हेतुना

Lakshmi said to Vishnu: With what purpose are you sleeping in the Milky Ocean?

नाहं सुमुखि निद्रालुर्निजं माहेश्वरं वपुः
दृशा तत्वानुवर्त्तिन्या पश्याम्यंतर्निमग्नया

कुशाग्रया धिया देवि यदंतर्योगिनो हृदि
पश्यंति यच्च वेदानां सारं मीमांसते भृशम्

तदेवमक्षरं ज्योतिरात्मरूपमनामयम्
अखंडानंद संदोह निष्पादि द्वैतवर्जितम्

यदाश्रया जगद्वृत्तिर्यन्मया चानुभूयते
न येन रहितं किंचिज्जगत्तत्वं चराचरम्

निर्मथ्य बहुधालोक्य वेदशास्त्रांबुधिं सुधीः
द्वैपायनो यदासाद्य गीताशास्त्रं निसृष्टवान्

यदास्थाय महानंदमानंदीकृतमानसः
निद्रालुरिव देवेशि दुग्धाब्धौ प्रतिभामि वै

इति तस्य मुरारातेर्मितमानंदवद्वचः
सा हर्षोत्फुल्ललोलाक्षी लक्ष्मी श्रुत्वा विसिस्मिरे

Vishnu said to Lakshmi: I am not sleeping in the Milky Ocean. I am focused inward and am trying to pursue and understand the ultimate truth Maheshvara who is in the heart of all the living entities. He (Bhagavan Shiva) whom the contemplative saints try to see in their hearts with their sharp intellect, who produces a continuous mass of joy, who is one without a second, is the immutable light, unharmed, resorting to whom the entire world subsists, without which there is no element in this world mobile or immobile, which is what is experienced by me. Experiencing that ultimate joy (through the grace of Lord Shiva) Vyasa the intelligent one, produced the Gita and the holy Vedas. I appear to be sleeping in the Milky Ocean, but my mind is delighted having resorted to that ultimate joy (meditating on Lord Shiva in the heart).

Padma Purana Uttara Khanda Chapter 175 Verses 14-18:

तस्मात्त्वत्तः परं यत्तच्छ्रोतुं कौतूहलं हि मे
चराचराणां लोकानां कर्त्ता हर्त्ता स्वयं प्रभुः
यथास्थितस्ततोऽन्यत्वं यदि मां बोधयाच्युत

Lakshmi asks to Vishnu: "I have a great curiosity to hear from you, about that which is higher than you. O Achyuta, tell me if there is something different from you who are the lord, the creator, and the destroyer of the worlds".

मायामयमिदं देवि वपुर्मे न तु तात्विकम्
सृष्टिस्थित्योपसंहारक्रियाजालोपबृंहितम्

अतोऽन्यदात्मनोरूपं द्वैताद्वैतविवर्जितम्
भावाभावविनिर्मुक्तमाद्यंतरहितं प्रिये

शुद्धसंवित्प्रभालाभं परानंदैकसुंदरम्
रूपमैश्वरमात्मैक्यगम्यं गीतासु कीर्तितम्

Vishnu replies to Lakshmi: O goddess, my body is not eternal (**it is bound to destruction**), and is augmented with the mass of the acts of creation, maintenance and withdrawal. The nature of the self is different from this. It is without duality and unity. It is free from existence and non-existence; without beginning or end. It is pure consciousness, has acquired luster, is beautiful due to great joy, is verily the form of Lord Shiva and it can be known only through realizing the inner soul (Lord Shiva) and this is what is told in the Gita.

Padma Purana Uttara Khanda Chapter 175 Verses 26-28: Vishnu goes on to say to Lakshmi that the entire Bhagavad Gita is the divine form of Lord Shiva.

शृणु सुश्रोणि वक्ष्यामि गीतासु स्थितिमात्मनः
वक्त्राणि पंच जानीहि पंचाध्यायाननुक्रमात्

दशाध्याया भुजाश्चैक उदरं द्वौ पदांबुजे
एवमष्टादशाध्याया वाङ्मयी मूर्तिरैश्वरी

विज्ञेया ज्ञानमात्रेण महापातकनाशिनी

shruNu sushroNi vakshyami gItAsu sthitimAtmanaha
vaktrANi pancha jAnIhi panchAdhyAyAn anukramAt

dashAdhyAyA bhujAschaika udaram dvau padAmbuje
evam ashtAdashAdhyAyA vAngmayI mUrtir aishvarI

vijnyeyA jnyAnamAtreNa mahApAtakanAshinI

I will tell you about my firm existence in the Gita. The five chapters are the five faces of Lord Shiva in order. The next ten chapters are the ten hands of Lord Shiva; one is the stomach, and the remaining two are the lotus feet of Lord Shiva. Thus the eighteen chapters are the divine form of Lord Shiva. By acquiring knowledge of it, all the great sins are destroyed.

Here Vishnu highlights that Bhagavad Gita is all about Lord Shiva and his divine form: SHUDHAH SPHATIKA SANKAASHAM PANCAVAKTRAKAM DASHA BHUJAM TRINETRAM - crystal white appearance, five faces, ten hands, three-eyes, etc.

Everywhere in the Vedas, Upanishads, Smritis, Puranas and Upa-Puranas, the five-faced, ten-handed form is described as that of Lord Shiva alone and not anyone else. We saw references from Garuda Purana, Yoga Tattva Upanishad & Yoga Yajna Valkya Smriti. Let's see some more references:

Varaha Purana Chapter 144 Verse 20:

शिवं सौम्यमुमाकान्तं भक्तानुग्रहकातरम् ।
नतोऽस्मि पंचवदनं नीलकण्ठं त्रिलोचनम् ।।

shivam saumyam umAkAntam bhakta anugrahakAtaram
natosmi panchavadanam nIlakanTam trilochanam

Chandra says to Lord Shiva: I bow to three-eyed, five-faced, blue-necked, Lord Shiva who is the lord of Uma, who is calm and eager to bless the devotees.

Padma Purana Kriya Yoga Sara Khanda Chapter 13 Verse 110: नमस्ते पंचवक्त्राय (namaste panchavaktrAya)

Brahmana says: Obeisances to five-faced Lord Shiva

Narada Purana Purva Bhaga Chapter 16 Verse 84: नमः पञ्चास्यदेवाय (namah panchAsya devAya)

Sage Bhagiratha says: Obeisances to five-faced Lord Shiva

Narada Purana Uttara Bhaga Chapter 73 Verse 42:

ईशान ते तत्पुरुष नमो घोराय ते सदा
वामदेव नमस्तेऽस्तु सद्योजाताय वै नमः

IshAna te tatpurusHa namo ghorAya te sadA
vAmadeva namastestu sadyojAtAya vai namaha

Sage Jaimini says to Lord Shiva: My prostrations to Sadyojaataa, Vaamadeva, Aghora, Tatpurusha, Ishaana.

Pancha Brahma Suktam from the Upanishads glorifies the five faces of Lord Shiva. There is a separate Upanishad called Pancha Brahma Upanishad which describes in detail the five faces of Lord Shiva.

There is a famous mantra for meditation usually recited before the chanting of the Shiva Sahasranaama which goes as:

shAntham padmAsanastham shashi dhara makutam pancha vakthram trinetram
shUlam vajram cha khaDgam parashum abhayadham dakshabhAge vahantham
nAgam pAsham cha gantam pralayahuthavaham sAnkusam vAma bhAge
nAnAlankAra yuktham sphatikamani nibham pArvathIsham namAmi

I salute the lord of Mother Parvathi, who is ever peaceful, who sits in the lotus pose, who wears the crescent on his crown, who has five faces, who has three eyes, who carries on his right side: trident, thunderbolt, sword, axe and sign of refuge, who carries on his left side: snake, rope, bell, fire and goad, who has been beautifully decorated and who is like crystal white in appearance.

FIVE FACED TEN HANDED FORM OF LORD SHIVA

So be it Bhagavad Gita of Mahabharata, Ishvara Gita of Kurma Purana, Shiva Gita of Padma Purana, etc. in all of them, the essence is Bhagavan Shiva alone and not anyone else. There are many more references from the scriptures to prove that Bhagavad Gita is a Shaivite scripture and many Shaiva Acharyas have given a commentary on the same.

We can see how Bhagavan Shiva is described as the essence of the Bhagavad Gita. Only by analyzing the scriptures as a whole, one can come to this conclusion, not otherwise. Some people having hatred for Mahadeva go to the extent of denigrating him. Liberation can never be obtained by those even in crores of births. This is told by Krishna himself his devotee Satyasandha.

Suta Samhita Yajna Vaibhava Khanda Purva Bhaga Chapter 25 Verses 52, 53:

mahAdevam vinA yo mAm bhajathe shraddhayA saha
nAsti tasya vinirmokshah samsArajanmakotibhihi

sarvamuktam samAsena mama bhaktasya tenagha
shivAd anyam parityajya shivam sAmbam sadA bhaja

Krishna says to Satyasandha: Casting aside Mahadeva, even if one worships me with faith, they would never attain liberation even in crores of births. So, casting aside everybody, worship & sing the praises of Lord Saamba Shiva alone.

So coming to the point, this divine form of Bhagavan Shiva along with Para Shakti sitting on his left lap is glorified in various places in the scriptures. But Mahadeva appears in various other forms like Ardhanaarishvara, Chidambara Nataraja, Thiruvaarur Thyagaraja, Kalyana Sundara Murthy, Uma Maheshvara, Somaa Skanda Murthy, Maha Sadashiva Murthy (25-faced), SadaShiva Murthy (5-faced, 10-handed), Chandrakshekara Murthy, Baala Shiva, Tripura Samhaara, etc. These forms are equally celebrated as direct forms of Parama Shiva.

In whatever way the individual soul wants to serve Lord Shiva, he/she will go back to Maha Kailasha (the highest spiritual world) and serve Shiva along with Shakti in that way. Akka Mahadevi had Maadhurya Bhaavam (husband-wife relationship, selfless love) for Lord Shiva, Bejja Mahadevi had Vaatsalya Bhaavam (motherly affection) for Lord Shiva, Maanickavaachagar, Nandanaar, Rudra Pashupati had Daasya Bhaavam (servant-master relationship) for Lord Shiva. Lord Shiva appears in that form for the pleasure of the devotees. But we need to understand that meditation should be done only on the forms of Lord Shiva who is the Supreme soul and not that of Brahma, Vishnu & Indra because they are individual souls (Jeevaatmaas) who are temporary.

Parama Shiva in Maha Kailasha becomes five-fold for creation, maintenance, destruction, concealment & liberation. He appears as SadaShiva for giving liberation, Maheshvara for concealment and Kaala Rudra for destruction. Brahma & Narayana are assigned the task of creation and maintenance. One point to be noted here is SadaShiva & Maheshvara have the complete spark of Parama Shiva in Maha Kailasha, Rudra who does the task of destruction has the partial spark of Parama Shiva whereas Brahma and Narayana are individual souls (Jeevaatmaas) who have acquired the positions of Brahma and Vishnu by saadhanaa (austerities to Lord Shiva). Brahma and Vishnu are positions that can be acquired by the Jeevaatmaa by saadhanaa. But a true devotee of Lord Shiva is not interested in the positions of Brahma & Hari as they are bound to destruction & change.

Mahabharata Anushaasana Parva Chapter 18 Verses 64, 65:

सदृशोऽरण्यवासीनां मुनीनां भावितात्मनाम्
ब्रह्मत्वं केशवत्वं वा शक्रत्वं वा सुरैः सह
त्रैलोक्यस्याधिपत्यं वा तुष्टो रुद्रः प्रयच्छति

sadrushoraNyavAsInAm munInAm bhAvitAtmanAm
brahmatvam keshvatvam vA shakratvam vA suraih saha
trailokyasyAdhipatyam vA tushto rudrah prayachhati

Sage Upamanyu says: If Lord Shiva is gratified with a person, he can grant the positions of Brahma, Keshava, Sakra and all the devatas or the sovereignty of the three worlds.

So worshipping the forms of Brahma, Hari, Indra & Lakshmi leads the individual soul (Jeevaatmaa) in taking repeated cycles of birth and death as they themselves belong to the Jiva tattva category.

Sage Vishvaanara describes Lord Shiva to be formless. Here one should understand that formless doesn't mean without a form **but without a material form**. Lord Shiva's form transcends all material forms. Our body is material that is bound by birth, old age, disease and death. Starting from the blade of grass to Vishnu everything is bound by birth, old age, disease and death. The divine spiritual body of Lord Shiva is ageless and is beyond all material forms. It is eternal, indestructible and imperishable. Even the Upanishads cannot comprehend the divine spiritual form of Lord Shiva and that's why sometimes he is described as formless because his form is not bound by birth, old age, disease or death and not bound by the three modes of material nature.

Through the radiant splendor coming out of his body, his presence can be felt everywhere. The Maayaavaadis describe the end goal as becoming consciousness → Jyoti which is nothing but the splendor coming out of the spiritual divine body of Lord Shiva who is eternal. According to them the Jiva, Jagat, Ishvara and everything is false. But that's not the case. The Jiva, Jagat and Ishvara are eternal and the Jiva & Jagat are controlled by Lord Shiva. There is a personality behind the splendor which is shown in the Upanishads:

Atharvashiras Upanishad:

यो वै रुद्रः स भगवान्यच्च तेजस्तस्मै वै नमोनमः

yo vai rudraH sa bhagavAnyachcha tejastasmai vai namonamaH

He who is Rudra is verily the Supreme Lord (bhagavAn). My salutations to Rudra who is the personification of infinite splendor.

Isha Upanishad Verse 15, Brihadaranyaka Upanishad 5.15.1:

हिरण्मयेन पात्रेण सत्यस्यापिहितं मुखम् ।
तत्त्वं पूषन्नपावृणुसत्यधर्माय दृष्टये॥

hiraNmayena pAtreNa satyasyApihitaM mukham
tattvaM pUShannapAvRiNu satyadharmAya dRiShTaye

O Ultimate Supreme Reality (or) Ultimate Supreme Being Saamba Shiva, your face is covered by your golden splendor. O Ultimate Protector, remove that and manifest your divine spiritual form to me.

Here Lord Shiva is described as having a golden splendor. His form is also described as golden in the Vedas, Upanishads, Puranas, etc. Some of the Upanishads where he is described as golden are: Mundaka, Chandogya, Taittiriya, Brihat Jabala, Bhasma Jabala, Isha, Brihadaaranyaka, Kaivalya, etc. He is the only personality who is described as golden in complexion, everywhere in the scriptures. He is also mentioned so in Shata Rudriyam (**namo hiranyabAhave**), Manu Smriti, etc. He alone is described as the golden Veda Purusha (**hiranmaya puruShaH, puruSho vai rudraH**). Brahma, Vishnu & Indra are not described as golden. The complexion of Lord Shiva itself describes him to be Shuddha Sattva (**pure mode of goodness**) which is beyond the 3 modes: mode of goodness, mode of passion and mode of ignorance and the creator of Brahma, Narayana, Kaala Rudra & Indra.

Isha Upanishad Verse 16, Brihadaranyaka Upanishad 5.15.1:

पूषन्नेकर्षे यम सूर्य प्राजापत्य व्यूह रश्मीन् ।
समूह तेजोयत्तेरूपं कल्याणतमं तत्तेपश्यामि योऽसावसौपुरुषः सोऽहमस्मि ॥

pUShannekarShe yama sUrya prAjApatya vyUha rashmIn
samUha tejo yatte rUpaM kalyANatamaM tatte pashyAmi yosAvasau puruShaH sohamasmi

O Lord Shiva, the sole controller of the entire universe. Please withdraw your golden splendor. By your grace, I wish to see that divine spiritual form of yours that has divine qualities & attributes. I am the eternal servant of that Ultimate Purusha Lord Shiva.

Meditating on the infinite Jyoti is not the highest meditation but meditating on the divine form of Bhagavan Shiva along with Para Shakti in the Jyoti is the highest meditation. Mahadeva appeared as an infinite pillar of fire (Agni Sthamba) to crush the ego of Brahma & Hari. But he has a divine spiritual form that should be contemplated upon within the Linga.

There is a place in the scriptures where Sage Dadhichi talks about the glories of Bhasma to all the sages. To bring about the greatness of Bhasma he recounts a story where Vishnu bathes with the sacred ash and eats the sacred ash to get the knowledge of Lord Shiva.

Padma Purana Paataala Khanda Chapter 105 Verse 218-233:

दधीच उवाच-
स्ववक्षः स्थितभस्मैकं नखेनादाय शंकरः
प्रणवेनाभिमंत्र्याथ गायत्र्या ब्रह्मभूतया

अंगुलिभ्यामुपादाय शिवः पंचाक्षरेण वै
हरिमस्तकगात्रेषु सर्वेष्वपि समाक्षिपत्

Sage Dadhichi said: Then Lord Shiva took scratched the sacred ash on Hari's chest with his nail, consecrated it with OM and Gayatri, took it with between his fingers, and with the five-syllabled hymn (NAMAH SHIVAAYA) he threw it on the head and all the limbs of Hari.

शांतदृष्ट्या निरीक्ष्याथ जीवेत्याह हरिं हरः
ध्यायस्व किं ते हृदये स च ध्यानपरोऽभवत्

अपश्यद्धृदये दीपं दीर्घाकारमतिप्रभम्
हरिराह शिवं साक्षाद्दीपो दृष्टो मयेति च

शिवः प्राह न ते ज्ञानं परिपक्वमथो हरे
भस्म भक्षय ते ज्ञानं समग्रं संभविष्यति

Gazing at him with tranquil eyes, Lord Shiva said to Vishnu: "Meditate on what is there in your heart". Then Vishnu was intent on meditation. In his heart, he saw a lamp (Jyoti) in a big shape and very bright. Vishnu said to Lord Shiva: "I have actually seen a lamp (Jyoti)". Shiva said: "O Vishnu, your knowledge is not mature. Eat the sacred ash. Then your knowledge will be complete".

Here an important thing to be noted is Vishnu meditates initially on the Jyoti which is nothing but the radiant splendor coming out of the spiritual divine body of Lord Shiva. It represents his infiniteness. Even though he had meditated on his splendor, Vishnu did not acquire complete knowledge. Vishnu then eats the sacred ash as per the order of Lord Shiva and then meditates in his heart.

पुनर्ध्यानपरो भूत्वा दीपमध्ये च पूरुषम्
शुद्धस्फटिकसंकाशं त्रिनेत्रं द्विभुजं शिवम्

वरदं दक्षिणे हस्ते वामे चाभयदं विभुम्
पंचवर्षीयवपुषं शरच्चंद्रायुतद्युतिम्

माणिक्यकुंडलं हेम दामजालविभूषितम्
रत्नांगुलीयसुभगं बाहुकोष्ठसुभूषणम्

तनुरक्तोष्ठमाकर्ण दीर्घायतविलोचनम्
बाणलोचनसंकाशं भाललोचनमव्ययम्

कंदर्पकार्मुकभ्रांतिजनकभ्रुवमीश्वरम्
स्निग्धोन्नत सुचार्वंग नासमच्छकपोलकम्

मंदस्मितं प्रसन्नास्यं बालेंदुदर्शनं विभुम्
विज्ञानरक्तवसनं वेदकल्पितनूपुरम्

वामांगुलीयमध्यस्थमतिप्रणवमव्ययम्
दृष्टवानथ तं विष्णुः कृतकृत्योऽभवत्तदा

अथाह शंभुर्भो विष्णो हृदि दृष्टं त्वया किमु
हरिराह पुरा दृष्टः पुरुषः शांतविग्रहः

इत्युदीर्य महाविष्णुः शिवपादे पपात ह

Vishnu became engrossed in meditation, and in the Jyoti (lamp), he saw a man who was like a pure crystal, who was Lord Shiva with three eyes and two hands, who gave a boon with the right hand and fearlessness with the left, whose body was like that of a child of five years, whose brilliance was like that of a myriad moons, whose ear-rings were made of emeralds, who was adorned with a row of necklaces, who was handsome due to a jeweled ring, who had put on ornaments on his arms and chest etc., whose lips were small and red, whose eyes were long and reached his ears, whose eyes were sharp like arrows, who had an eye on his forehead, who was immutable, whose eyebrows created the illusion of Cupid's bow, who was the Supreme Lord, whose lovely nose was high, whose cheeks were spotless, whose smile was gentle, whose face was pleased, who looked like the young moon, who was mighty, who had put on the red garment of wisdom, who had devised the anklets of the Vedas, who had put a jeweled OM in the left finger and who was immutable. Then Vishnu became blessed. Then Shambhu said: "O Vishnu, what did you see in your heart?" Vishnu said: "First I saw a man of a gentle body." Saying so, Vishnu fell at the feet of Lord Shiva.

After realizing it is none other than Lord Shiva who is the inner soul (**antaryAmi**) of everyone, Vishnu surrenders to Lord Shiva and glorifies the sacred ash and Lord Shiva (**namastestu namastestu tvAmaham sharaNam gataH**)

So here the conclusion is Vishnu acquired complete knowledge after meditating on the divine spiritual form of Lord Shiva within the Jyoti. Likewise, the Linga represents his infiniteness. But the highest form of meditation is meditating on the form of Parama Shiva within the Linga which even devatas like Brahma, Hari & Indra do. This is also connected with the Upanishads as quoted before where Mahadeva's infiniteness is spoken first and then the Upanishads go on to describe the beautiful form of the Supreme Lord Shiva which is filled with divine qualities, attributes & characteristics which is covered by golden splendor.

CHAPTER 3
Triad - Individual soul, Supreme soul, the universe

VERSE 3:

रज्जौ सर्पः शुक्तिकायां च रूप्यं नैरःपूरस्तन्मृगाख्ये मरीचौ ।
यद्वत्तद्वद्विष्वगेष प्रपंचो यस्मिञ्ज्ञाते तं प्रपद्ये महेशम् ।।

rajjau sarpaH shuktikAyAM ca rUpyaM nairaH pUrastan mrugAkye marIchau |
yadvat tadvad vishvagesha prapancho yasmin jnyaate taM prapadye mahesham ||

The snake in the rope, the silver in the oyster shell, the water in the mirage - just like that when Lord Shiva is known, the whole world vanishes (the bondage with the whole world vanishes) and Truth alone remains. I resort to that great Lord Maheshvara.

COMMENTARY:

We have to understand this verse very carefully because Maayaavaadis (followers of Adi Shankara who are prachanna bauddhas → covered Buddhists) are known for misinterpreting this verse.

Let us analyze some aphorisms from the Upanishads:

1) **Maha Narayana Upanishad:**

सर्वो वैरुद्रस्तस्मैरुद्राय नमो अस्तु । पुरुषोवैरुद्रः सन्महोनमोनमः ।
विश्वं भूतं भुवनं चित्रं बहुधा जातं जायमानं च यत् । सर्वो ह्येष रुद्रस्तस्मैरुद्राय नमो अस्तु ॥

sarvo vai rudrastasmai rudrAya namo astu
puruSho vai rudraH sanmaho namo namaH
vishvaM bhUtaM bhuvanam chitraM bahudhA jAtam jAyamAnam cha yat
sarvo hyeSha rudrastasmai rudrAya namo astu

All this is verily Rudra (Parama Shiva). To Rudra who is the Supreme Reality, we offer our salutation. We salute again and again that Being, Rudra, who alone is the light and the Soul of creatures. The material universe, the created beings and whatever there is manifoldly present and profusely created in the past and in the present in the form of the world, all that is indeed Rudra. Salutations be to Rudra who is such.

Chandogya 3.14.1:

सर्वं खल्विदं ब्रह्म तज्जलानिति शान्त उपासीत

sarvaM khalvidaM brahma tajjalAniti shAnta upAsIta

Verily, **all this is Brahman (Lord Shiva)**. From him, everything originates and into him, they dissolve and by him, everything is sustained. One should meditate on him alone in tranquillity.

Shvetashvatara Upanishad 3.11:

सर्वव्यापी स भगवांस्तस्मात् सर्वगतः शिवः ॥

sarvavyApI sa bhagavAMstasmAt sarvagataH shivaH

Bhagavan Shiva is the **all-pervading Lord**. He is omnipresent and benevolent.

Atharvashiras Upanishad:

स सर्वव्यापी यः सर्वव्यापी सोऽनन्तः योऽनन्त

sa sarvavyApI yaH sarvavyApI so anantaH yo ananta

He is **All-Pervading and Infinite**.

2) **Maha Narayana Upanishad (The same verse comes with a slight modification in Shvetashvatara Upanishad 3.4, Shvetashvatara Upanishad 4.12):**

योदेवानां प्रथमं पुरस्ताद्विश्वाधिकोरुद्रोमहर्षिः ।
हिरण्यगर्भं पश्यत जायमानꣳ स नोदेवः शुभयास्मृत्या संयुनक्तु ॥

yo devAnAM prathamaM purastAd vishvAdhiko rudro maharShiH hiraNyagarbhaM pashyata jAyamAnam sa no devaH shubhayA smRityA samyunaktu

May the omniscient Rudra who is **superior to the universe**, who has been revealed in the Vedas, who is the Supreme Seer, who gave birth to Hiranyagarbha (Brahma), who is the first among the gods and who is born before all the rest endow us with clear intellect.

Bhasma Jabala Upanishad:

सोमोऽहमेव जनिता विश्वाधिको रुद्रो महर्षिः हिरण्यगर्भादीनहं जायमानान्पश्यामि

somo ahameva janitA vishvAdhiko rudro maharShiH hiraNyagarbhAdInahaM jAyamAnAnpashyAmi

Parama Shiva says: "I along with Para Shakti (SHIVA + UMA → SOMA) create everything and I am the **Great Seer superior to the universe** who gave birth to Hiranyagarbha."

3) **Maha Narayana Upanishad:**

कद्रुद्राय प्रचेतसेमीढुष्टमाय तव्यसे ।
वोचेम शंतमꣳ हृदे । सर्वोह्येष रुद्रस्तस्मैरुद्राय नमोअस्तु ॥

kadrudrAya prachetase mIDhuShTamAya tavyase

vochema shantamam hRide sarvohyeSha rudrastasmai rudrAya namo astu

We sing a hymn to Rudra who provides the highest happiness and who is the only worthy of praise, who is omniscient, who rains his grace to the worshippers most excellently, who is the most powerful and who **is dwelling in the heart of the all the living entities and devatas**. Indeed all this is Rudra. Salutations be to Rudra who is such.

RUDRAM Anuvaaka 9 (Krishna Yajur Veda Taittiriya Samhita 4th Canto 5th Chapter), Shukla Yajur Veda Vaajasaneyi Samhita 16.46: देवाना॑ᳵ हृदयेभ्यो

devAnAgum hridayebhyo

He resides **in the heart of all the devatas and living entities**.

Shvetashvatara Upanishad 3.13 (The same verse comes with a slight modification in Katha Upanishad 2.3.17, Shvetashvatara Upanishad 4.17):

अङ्गुष्ठमात्रः पुरुषोऽन्तरात्मा सदा जनानां हृदये सन्निविष्टः
हृदा मनीषा मनसाभिक्लृप्तो य एतद् विदुरमृतास्तेभवन्ति

aNguShThamAtraH puruSho antarAtmA sadA janAnAM hRidaye sanniviShTaH
hRidA manIShA manasAbhiklipto ya etad viduramRitAste bhavanti

Lord Shiva the Ultimate Purusha in the size of a thumb**, is present as the inner self in the heart of all the living entities**. They who know Him become immortal (attain liberation).

Atharvashikha Upanishad:

कारणं कारणानां ध्याता कारणं तु ध्येयः सर्वैश्वर्यसम्पन्नः शंभुराकाशमध्ये

kAraNam kAraNAnAm dhyAtA kAraNam tu dhyeyaH sarvaishvaryasampannaH shaMbhurAkAshamadhye

The cause of all the causes alone should be meditated upon. Shambhu, who is the Supreme Lord of all, possessed of all powers like Omniscience, Omnipotence and endowed with all the perfections is to be meditated in the ether (**Hridayaakaasha or Daharaakaasha**) of the middle of the heart.

From the above aphorisms, we see that, in the first set of aphorisms, Lord Shiva is described as all-pervading, in the second set of aphorisms, Lord Shiva is described as beyond the universe and in the third set of aphorisms, Lord Shiva is described as being present in the heart of all the living entities (individual souls). Aphorisms supporting Advaitha, Dvaita, Dvaitaadvaita, etc. are present in the Vedas & Upanishads. So in this case, when we want to come to an inference, we have to correlate all the aphorisms in the Vedas & Upanishads and we cannot pick selective aphorisms and come to a final conclusion. Maayaavaadis take the aphorisms that talk about non-difference alone and say Advaitha is the final philosophy. But there are many number of aphorisms talking about the difference between the individual soul and the Supreme soul. How can one discard those aphorisms and try to make a final conclusion? When we analyze the aphorisms in the Upanishads with the help of supporting facts from the Puranas, we can understand that both difference & non-difference is spoken of between the individual soul & Supreme soul.

The concept of triad - JIVA, JAGAT & ISHVARA i.e. PASHU, PAASHAM & PATHI is explained in various places in the Upanishads & Puranas.

Isha Upanishad Verse 1:

ॐ ईशा वास्यमिदꣳ सर्वं यत्किञ्च जगत्यां जगत् ।

AUM IshA vAsyamidagum sarvaM yatkincha jagatyAM jagat

Whatever exists in this changing universe animate or inanimate is under the control of Parama Shiva.

Shvetashvatara Upanishad Chapter 1 Verse 12:

भोक्ता भोग्यं प्रेरितारं च मत्वा

bhoktA bhogyaM preritAraM cha matvA

The enjoyer (Jeevaatmaa → individual Soul), the object of enjoyment (Jagat → Universe) and the Ruler (Ishvara → Supreme Lord).

Atharvashiras Upanishad:

रुद्रो हि शाश्वतेन वै पुराणेनेषमूर्जेण तपसा नियन्ता अग्निरिति भस्म वायुरिति भस्म जलमिति भस्म स्थलमिति भस्म व्योमेति भस्म
सर्वंह वा इदं भस्म मन एतानि चक्षूंषि यस्माद्व्रतमिदं पाशुपतं यद्भस्म नाङ्गानि संस्पृशेत्तस्माद्ब्रह्म तदेतत्पाशुपतं पशुपाश विमोक्षणाय

rudro hi shAshvatena vai purANeneShamUrjeNa tapasA niyantA agniriti bhasma vAyuriti bhasma jalamiti bhasma sthalamiti bhasma vyometi bhasma sarvamha vA idaM bhasma mana etAni chakShUmShi yasmAdvratamidaM pAshupataM yadbhasma nANgAni samspRishettasmAdbrahma tadetatpAshupataM pashupAsha vimokShaNAya

One should reach Rudra, by Tapas (meditation), who is Eternal, Ancient, and the Giver of strength. The following is called Paashupata vow. "**Fire is Bhasma, Wind is Bhasma, Water is Bhasma, Earth is Bhasma, Ether is Bhasma. All this is Bhasma. And mind and all the senses are Bhasma**". By this hymn taking the holy ashes, mixing them with water, one should besmear himself all over. One should observe this vow called Paashupata **for the sake of getting rid of the noose (Paasha → bondage) of the Pashu (Jeevaatmaa → individual soul)**.

Bhasma Jabala Upanishad:

ध्यात्वा साम्बं मामेव वृषभारूढं हिरण्यबाहुं हिरण्यवर्णं हिरण्यरूपं
पशुपाशविमोचकं पुरुषं कृष्णपिङ्गलमूर्ध्वरेतं विरूपाक्षं विश्वरूपं

dhyAtvA sAmbaM mAmeva vRiShabhArUDhaM
hiraNyabAhuM hiraNyavarNaM hiraNyarUpaM
pashupAshavimochakaM puruShaM kRiShNapiNgalam
UrdhvaretaM virUpAkShaM vishvarUpaM

Lord Shiva says: One should meditate on me alone who is with Uma, who is sitting on the sacred bull, with golden arms, with golden complexion and golden form, **who is the remover of the noose of the Pashus (the ignorant Jivas)**, who is the Purusha, with dark and golden (Uma Maheshvara), highest of all, uncommon eyes (three-eyed) and whose form is the universe.

SHIVA KAAMA SUNDARI ALONG WITH CHIDAMBARA NATARAAJAA

विश्वेश्वरोऽहमजरोऽहम् । मामेवं विदित्वा संसृतिपाशात्प्रमुच्यते । तस्मादहं **पशुपाशविमोचकः** । पशवश्चामानवान्तं मध्यवर्तिनश्च युक्तात्मानो यतन्ते मामेव प्राप्तुम् । प्राप्यन्ते मां न पुनरावर्तन्ते ।

vishveshvaroham ajaroham mAmevaM viditvA samsRitipAshAtpramuchyate tasmAdahaM **pashupAshavimochakaH** pashavashchAmAnavAntaM madhyavartinashcha yuktAtmAno yatante mAmeva prAptum prApyante mAM na punarAvartante

Lord Shiva says: I am the lord of everything and am immortal. Thus realizing me one is freed from the bondage of Samsara. **Therefore I am the remover of the noose of the Pashus**. The Pashus who are the devatas (Brahma, Hari, Indra, etc.) and humans, with concentrated minds, are making effort to reach me only. They who reach me never come back (to the worldly life), never come back.

From the above aphorisms in the Upanishads, we can confirm that JIVA, JAGAT & ISHVARA i.e. PASHU, PAASHAM & PATHI are true (SATHYAM) and eternal (NITHYAM). Jagat Mithya (the world is an illusion) which is stated by the Maayaavaadis is not entertained as it is contradictory to the statements in the Upanishads. The PASHUS refer to the individual souls starting from the blade of grass to Vishnu. PAASHAM is the bondage with the world that the Jeevaatmaa has (repeated cycles of births and deaths). The PATHI is the Lord who is otherwise called PASHUPATHI who takes away the PAASHAM (bondage with the universe) and liberates the PASHU (Jeevaatmaa).

When the individual soul (Jeevaatmaa) looks at everything in this world as belonging to the Supreme Reality Parama Shiva, who is also present in the heart of all the living entities & the devatas and also who is present beyond the universe and when the Jeevaatmaa starts utilizing everything in the service of Parama Shiva then the Jeevaatmaa is freed from all bondage with the world and goes back to Maha Kailasha (highest place) and doesn't return from there.

This is supported by the below aphorism which comes 6 times in Shvetashvatara Upanishad:

ज्ञात्वा देवं मुच्यते सर्वपाशैः (**Shvetashvatara Upanishad 1.8, 1.11, 4.15, 4.16, 5.13, 6.13**)

jnyAtvA devaM muchyate sarvapAshaiH

The Jeevaatmaa (individual soul) after realizing the Supreme soul is freed from all bondage.

Here the word Paasha (bondage) is used 6 times in Shvetashvatara Upanishad which is also mentioned in other Upanishads & Puranas that refer to Pashu, Pathi & Paasham. As mentioned before, Sage Shvetashvatara is identified as a Shiva Bhakta in the Puranas and not as a devotee of Brahma or Hari.

When the Jeevaatmaa realizes that whatever it goes behind in this world i.e. name, fame, wealth, knowledge, beauty, power, etc. is temporary and also realizes that everything starting from the blade of grass till Vishnu is bound to destruction and Mahadeva is the only resort to attain liberation from the repeated cycles of birth and death then Mahadeva himself who is in the heart of the individual soul directs the soul to a proper Shaiva Guru belonging to an authorized Vaidika (upholding the Veda as the Supreme) Shaiva Sampradaya to take Diksha (spiritual initiation). Without the grace of a GURU, one can never attain Parama Shiva, not even in crores of births. The glory of GURU is told in the Upanishads:

Shvetashvatara Upanishad 6.23:

यस्य देवे परा भक्तिः यथा देवे तथा गुरौ ।
तस्यैते कथिता ह्यर्थाः प्रकाशन्ते महात्मनः ॥

yasya deve parA bhaktiH yathA deve tathA gurau
tasyaite kathitA hyarthAH prakAshante mahAtmanaH

These truths when taught shine forth only in that high-souled one who has supreme devotion to Parama Shiva and an equal degree of devotion to the Spiritual GURU. They shine forth in that high-souled one only.

Kaivalya Upanishad 5:

अन्त्याश्रमस्थः सकलेन्द्रियाणि निरुध्य भक्त्या स्वगुरुं प्रणम्य ॥
उमासहायं परमेश्वरं प्रभुं त्रिलोचनं नीलकण्ठं प्रशान्तम्
ध्यात्वा मुनिर्गच्छति भूतयोनिं समस्तसाक्षिं तमसः परस्तात्

antyAshramasthaH sakalendriyANi nirudhya bhaktyA svaguruM praNamya
umAsahAyaM parameshvaraM prabhuM trilochanaM nIlakaNThaM prashAntam
dhyAtvA munirgachChati bhUtayoniM samastasAkShiM tamasaH parastAt

Observing the vow of Atyaashrama, with all the senses under control, prostrating with devotion to the GURU, one has to meditate on Uma's spouse, the one who is eternally present with Uma, Para Shakti, Ambika (umAsahAyam); the supreme Lord (parameshvaraM); who is the Lord of the entire universe (prabhuM); the three-eyed (trilochanaM); the blue-necked lord (nilakantham); peaceful & benevolent (prashAntam), by meditating on this personality a Sage reaches Him (goes to the highest world Maha Kailasha and doesn't return from there) who is the origin of all beings, the witness of all and who is beyond darkness.

Here, in Kaivalya Upanishad Atyaashrama vow is spoken of which is also mentioned in the Shvetashvatara 6.21 (**atyAshramibhyaH paramaM pavitraM**). We also saw in the commentary to the first verse, how Sage Shvetashvatara is described as practicing the **Paashupata vow (or) Atyaashrama vow** which means one and the same.

Kurma Purana 1.14.32-33 (Same is told in Saura Purana 27.23-24 with a slight modification):

अथास्मिन्नन्तरेऽपश्यत् तमायान्तं महामुनिम् ।
श्वेताश्वतरनामानं महापाशुपतोत्तमम् ।।

भस्मसंदिग्धसर्वाङ्गं कौपीनाच्छादनान्वितम् ।
तपसा कर्षितात्मानं शुक्लयज्ञोपवीतिनम् ।।

athAsmin anatarepashyat tamAyAntam mahAmunim
shvetAshvataranAmAnam mahApAshupata uthamam

bhasmasamdigdhasavAngam kaupInAchhAdanAnvitam
tapasA karsHitAtmAnam shukla yajnyopavItinam

Sushila saw the great sage Shvetashvatara approaching. The sage Shvetashvatara was the most excellent among the devotees of Pashupati. He had applied Bhasma (holy ashes) all over his body. His body was emaciated due to the performance of penance. He was wearing a white sacred thread.

Kurma Purana 1.14.37-39:

सोऽनुगृह्याथ राजानं सुशीलं शीलसंयुतम्
शिष्यत्वे परिजग्राह तपसा क्षीणकल्पषम्

ददौ तदैश्वरं ज्ञानं स्वशाखाविहितं व्रतम्
अशेषवेदसारं तत् पशुपाशविमोचनम्

अन्त्याश्रममिति ख्यातं ब्रह्मादिभिरनुष्ठितम्

sonugruhyAtha rAjAnam sushIlam shIlasamyutam
shisHyatve parijagrAha tapasA kshINakalpasHam

dadau tad aishvaram jnyAnam svashAkhAvihitam vratam
ashesHvedasAram tat pashupAshavimochanam

antyAshramam iti khyAtam brahmAdibhir anushTitam

Sage Shvetashvatara blessed King Sushila who had very good conduct and gentle behavior. He accepted him as his disciple, for he had wiped off all his sins. Sage Shvetashvatara bestowed the divine knowledge about Lord Shiva to Sushila for which the holy rites had been laid down in the branch of the Vedas (Paashpata Vow & Atyaashrama Vow mean one and the same). Sage Shvetashvatara gave him the entire essence of the Vedas, which secures the release of the Pashu (individual soul) from the Paasha (bondage). It is famous as **Atyaashrama**. It has been performed by Brahma, Vishnu and others.

Here we see King Sushila's sins were completely removed by the grace of his GURU Sage Shvetashvatara. It is very important to surrender to a GURU to attain Lord Shiva.

Mundaka Upanishad 1.2.12:

तद्विज्ञानार्थं स गुरुमेवाभिगच्छेत् समित्पाणिः श्रोत्रियं ब्रह्मनिष्ठम् ॥

tadvijnyAnArthaM sa gurumevAbhigachChet samitpANiH shrotriyaM brahmaniShTham

In order to understand that Eternal, let him, fuel in hand, approach a GURU who is well versed in the Vedas and always devoted to Saguna Brahman (Parama Shiva).

Here the phrase "fuel in hand" is mentioned in the case of a disciple because the GURU has the fire to ignite the fuel by giving Shiva Jnyaanam (knowledge about Bhagavan Shiva) to the disciple and initiating him by giving Shiva Diksha. Shiva

Diksha is very important to attain Mahadeva without which one can never attain Bhagavan Shiva in crores of births.

So when one realizes that everything else is temporary and Mahadeva is the end goal, then one should quickly approach a Vaidika Shaiva GURU who is a practiser of Paashupata (or) Atyaashrama vow and take proper spiritual initiation under the GURU and also spread the glory of Lord Shiva to others as the Upanishads say **svAdhyAya pravachane cha**. One should know about the glories of Lord Shiva and also spread the glories of Lord Shiva. That is the highest service that one can do to GURU and the Supreme Lord Parama Shiva.

So here in this verse when Sage Vishvaanara says the whole world vanishes we should not be confused with the Maayaavaadi's interpretation of Jagat Mithyatvaa (the world is an illusion). The material world is temporary and not illusory. Saying that everything is illusory is an excuse given by the Maayaavaadis to prove their covered Buddhist philosophy as the right philosophy. According to the Maayaavaadis, everything is Mithya (false) including Jiva, Jagat and Ishvara. They go to the extent of saying even Veda Vaakyams (aphorisms from the Vedas) are false. How can Veda Vaakyams (aphorisms in the Vedas) which is the ultimate knowledge to understand Maheshvara be false? So that is not the right interpretation.

Sage Vishvaanara actually means that when the soul realizes Parama Shiva, the individual soul's bondage with the universe disappears and the individual soul eternally goes back to Maha Kailasha and engages in eternal service to Parama Shiva and Para Shakti and does not return from there.

CHAPTER 4
The individual soul is always dependent on Lord Shiva

VERSE 4:

तोये शैत्यं दाहकत्वं च वह्नौ तापो भानौ शीतभानौ प्रसादः ।
पुष्पे गंधो दुग्धमध्येपि सर्पिर्यत्तच्छंभो त्वं ततस्त्वां प्रपद्ये ।।

toye shaityaM dAhakatvaM cha vahnau tApo bhAnau shItabhAnau prasAdaH |
puShpe gandho dugdhamadhyepi sarpiryattat shambho tvaM tatastvAM prapadye ||

Coolness in the water, heat in the fire, the scorching nature in the sun and the pleasing gentleness in the moon, fragrance in the flower and the ghee in the milk. In that manner, O Parama Shiva, you are the essence in the world. Hence I resort only to you.

COMMENTARY:

An important point is highlighted by Sage Vishvaanara in this verse. Two things are described: the Fire and the heat from the fire, the Sun and the scorching rays of the sun. Through the rays of the sun, we experience the sunlight but the real SUN is a million miles far away. In one way we can say that the rays of the sun are non-different from the Sun but still the SUN is the source and is different from it's rays or the radiance that originates from the SUN. The Jeevaatmaas (individual souls) are like the sun's rays and Lord Shiva is like the sun. Just like the sun and the sun's rays are different, likewise, the Jeevaatmaas (individual souls) are always different from Paramaatmaa (Supreme Soul → Lord Shiva). Even at the time of liberation, the individual soul is separate from Lord Shiva. Though Lord Shiva is present in Maha Kailasha being served by crores of liberated souls (Mukta Jivas) still he is present as the inner soul of all the living entities present in the material universe. He alone is the ultimate witness & Sarvajnya (all-knowing). This message is nicely conveyed by Sage Vishvaanara.

Shvetashvatara Upanishad 1.10:

क्षरं प्रधानममृताक्षरं हरः क्षरात्मानावीशते देव एकः ।

kSharaM pradhAnam amRitAkSharaM haraH kSharAtmAnAvIshate deva ekaH

Prakriti is perishable. Hara, the Supreme Lord Shiva, is immortal and imperishable. The Supreme Lord Shiva doesn't have an equal and rules over both Prakriti and the individual souls.

Shvetashvatara Upanishad 4.6-7, Mundaka Upanishad 3.1.1-2:

द्वा सुपर्णा सयुजा सखाया समानं वृक्षं परिषस्वजाते ।
तयोरन्यः पिप्पलं स्वाद्वत्त्यन- श्नन्नन्यो अभिचाकशीति ॥

dvA suparNA sayujA sakhAyA samAnaM vRikShaM pariShasvajAte |
tayoranyaH pippalaM svAdvattyana shnannanyo abhichAkashIti ||

Two birds who are inseparable friends reside on the same tree. Of these, one eats the fruits of the tree and relishes them, while the other looks on without eating.

समाने वृक्षे पुरुषो निमग्नोऽ- नीशया शोचति मुह्यमानः ।
जुष्टं यदा पश्यत्यन्यमीशमस्य महिमानमिति वीतशोकः ॥

samAne vRikShe puruSho nimagno nIshayA shochati muhyamAnaH |
juShTaM yadA pashyatyanyamIshamasya mahimAnamiti vItashokaH ||

Sitting on the same tree the individual soul gets entangled and feels miserable, being deluded on account of forgetting it's true nature (**The nature of every individual soul is that, it is the eternal servant of Saamba Shiva**). When the individual soul sees the Supreme Lord of all, who is worshipped by everyone and realizes that all greatness is His, then the individual soul is relieved of all misery & bondage.

In the above aphorisms mentioned, the individual soul and the Supreme Lord are clearly identified as different. **Only when the individual soul realizes the Supreme Lord then it gets released from the repeated shackles of birth & death. Liberation is not about saying Jeevaas & Jagat are Mithya (illusion). It is about true surrender to the Supreme Lord Shiva.** The Supreme Lord is always independent whereas the individual soul is always dependent on the Supreme Lord.

Skanda Purana Arunaachala Mahatmya Uttaraardha Chapter 21 Verses 15, 16:

पाथोधिपोऽहं वीचिस्त्वं प्रकृतिस्त्वं पुमानहम् ।।
विद्या त्वं वेदितव्योऽहं वाक्त्वमर्थोपि पार्वती ।।

pAthodhipoham vIchistvam prakrutistvam pumAnaham
vidyA tvam veditavyoham vAktvam arthopi pArvati

Lord Shiva said to mother Parvathi: O dear, you are the wave, I am the ocean. You are Prakriti and I am Purusha. You are knowledge and I am the known. O Parvathi, you are the word and I am the connotation.

Linga Purana Canto 2 Chapter 11 Verses 4-5:

पुरुषं शंकरं प्राहुर्गौरीं च प्रकृतिं द्विजाः ।
अर्थः शंभुः शिवा वाणी दिवसोऽजः शिवा निशा ।।

सप्ततंतुर्महादेवो रुद्राणी दक्षिणा स्मृता ।
आकाशं शंकरो देवः पृथिवी शंकरप्रिया ।।

purusHam shankaram prAhur gaurIm cha prakrutim dvijAhA
artham shambhuh shivA vANI divasojah shivA nishA

saptatamtur mahAdevo rudrANI dakshiNA smrutA

AkAsham shankaro devah pruthivI shankarapriyA

The learned ones call Purusha as Lord Shiva and Prakriti as Mother Parvathi. Lord Shiva is the meaning and Parvathi is the word denoting the meaning. Lord Shiva is the day and Parvathi is the night. Lord Shiva is the lord of sacrifice and his consort is the gift offered in the sacrifice. Lord Shiva is the firmament and his beloved is the earth.

We see similar Puranic passages where mother Parvathi is described as the **knowledge to know Lord Shiva** and Parama Shiva is described as the **object of knowledge** just like we saw the example of heat from fire and rays from the sun.

But one should understand that Mother Parvathi (or) Ambika (or) Uma (or) Para Shakti (or) Lalitha Tripurasundari is eternal like Parama Shiva. She is Shakti (Power) and Mahadeva is Shakimaan (Embodiment of Power). Everything is under their control. The sum substance of the Jeevaatmaas starting from the blade of grass till Brahma, Vishnu, Lakshmi are under the control of Para Shakti and Parama Shiva. The entire world movable and immovable exist by their grace only. Para Shakti is Nithya Ishvari (eternal Goddess), Parama Shiva is Nithya Ishvara (eternal God). It is only by her grace we attain Parama Shiva. She gives the knowledge through which we get to know the object of knowledge (Parama Shiva).

Atharvashiras Upanishad:

अपाम सोमममृता अभूमागन्म

apAma somamamRitA abhUmAganma

The devatas say: After realizing the SOMA (Shiva + UMA) we have become immortal. We have reached the ultimate.

Atharvashikha Upanishad:

यावसानेऽस्य चतुर्थ्यर्धमात्रा सा सोमलोक ओङ्कारः

yAvasAne asya chaturthy ardhamAtrA sA somaloka omkAraH

The fourth is the sound of Ardhamaatra (that comes after reciting AUM) which is hidden. It represents OMKARA and it is the world of SOMA (SHIVA + UMA → SOMA, refers to Maha Kailasha the place where Para Shakti & Parama Shiva reside being served by crores of Mukta Jivas and which is the highest world that one can attain).

Kaivalya Upanishad: उमासहायं परमेश्वरं प्रभुं

umAsahAyaM parameshvaraM prabhuM

Uma's spouse, the one who is eternally present with Uma, Para Shakti, Ambika (umAsahAyam); the supreme Lord (parameshvaraM); who is the Lord of the entire universe (prabhuM).

RUDRAM Anuvaaka 8 (Krishna Yajur Veda Taittiriya Samhita 4th Canto 5th Chapter), Shukla Yajur Veda Vaajasaneyi Samhita 16.39: नमः सोमाय च रुद्राय च

namah somAya cha rudrAya cha

Salutations to him who is the consort of Uma and to him who removes all the sorrows.

Maha Narayana Upanishad:

नमो हिरण्यबाहवे हिरण्यवर्णाय हिरण्यरूपाय हिरण्यपतये
अम्बिकापतय उमापतये पशुपतये नमोनमः

namo hiraNyabAhave hiraNyavarNAya hiraNyarUpAya hiraNyapataye ambikApataya umApataye pashupataye namo namaH

Salutations again and again to Hiranyabahu (He whose hands are golden; one who has golden ornaments worn on his arms), Hiranyavarna (He whose complexion is golden), Hiranyarupa (He whose form is shining in golden splendor), Hiranyapati (the Lord of riches & all kinds of prosperity), Ambikapati (the consort of Ambika, the Mother of the entire universe), Umapati (The consort and the master of Uma), Pasupati (the Lord of all individual souls).

The Puranas clearly describe that the name UMA comes from OMKAARAM only. Mother UMA is Omkaareshvari (the Goddess of OMKAARAM) and Lord SHIVA is Omkaareshvara (the Lord of OMKAARAM).

Padma Purana Svarga Khanda Chapter 34 Verse 9-11: Sage Narada says to Yudhishtra:

ॐकारेश्वरमुत्तमम् कृत्तिवासेश्वरं लिंगं मध्यमेश्वरमुत्तमम्
विश्वेश्वरं तथोंकारंकंदर्पेश्वरमेव च

एतानि गुह्यलिंगानि वाराणस्यां युधिष्ठिर
न कश्चिदिह जानाति विना शंभोरनुग्रहात्

omkAreshvaram uthamam kruthivAseshvaram lingam madhyameshvaram uthamam
vishveshvaram tat omkAram kandarpeshvaram eva cha

etAni guhyalingAni vArANasyAm yudhishTira
na kaschidiha jAnAti vinA shambhor anugrahAt

The Omkaareshvara is the most excellent. There are Lingas called Krittivaaseshvara, the excellent Madhyameshvara, Vishveshvara, Omkaara and

Kandharpeshvara. O Yudhishtra, these are the secret Lingas in Kaashi (Vaaraanasi). No one experiences destruction here due to Shambhu's favor.

Kena Upanishad 3.12: उमाँ हैमवतीं

umAm haimavatIM

She was Uma, the daughter of the Himavan

Kena Upanishad 4.1: ब्रह्मणो वा एतद्विजये महीयध्वमिति

brahmaNo vA etadvijaye mahIyadhvamiti

Uma said to the Devatas: "Through the victory of **Brahman (Lord Shiva)** alone have you attained glory, not otherwise."

When the Devatas were bound by EGO thinking that they were the cause of victory over the demons, Para Shakti comes and explains that it is Lord Shiva who is the cause of their victory and none else.

There is a hymn that was sung by Sage Jaimini after seeing Mahadeva doing the Tandava (dance) at Sage Jaimini's request. When Sage Jaimini saw Lord Shiva doing the Tandava he couldn't control his ecstasy and he sang beautiful 113 verses starting from Verses 29 - 141 which is in the Narada Uttara Bhaga Chapter 73 - **The Greatness of Tryambakeshvara**. That hymn is called **Veda Paada**; meaning every verse contains a Paada from the Veda Upanishad Mantras. Each of the 113 verses sung by Sage Jaimini has a beautiful Vedantic import and it's very special, hence it is called Veda Paada.

Narada Uttara Bhaga Chapter 73 Verse 141: Sage Jaimini ends the Veda Paada hymn by saying:

शिवे कथं त्वत्समता क्व दीयते जगत्कृतिः केलिरयं शिवः पतिः ।

हरिस्तु दासोऽनुचरीन्दिरा शची सरस्वतीं वा सुभगा ददिर्वसु ।।

shive katham tvatsamatA kva dIyate jagatkrutih kelirayam shivah patihi
haristu dAsah anucharI indira shachI sarasvatIm vA subhagA dadirvasu

O Para Shakti & Parama Shiva, where and how can your equality be extended to? The creation of the entire universe is your sport. Hari is your servant. Lakshmi is your maidservant. So also are Sarasvathi & Indrani (wife of Indra). You both are the fortunate bestower of wealth on everybody.

So PARAMA SHIVA is the Supreme Lord and PARA SHAKTI is the Supreme Goddess. Apart from them, everybody including Brahma, Hari, Indra, Lakshmi, Sarasvathi & Indrani belongs to the JIVA Tattva (individual soul) category who are bound by birth, old age, disease, death & change.

Sage Vishvaanara ends by saying Lord Shiva is the essence of the world. He alone is the controller of all the individual souls & the entire universe. He is described as the essence of the Shruti (Vedas & Upanishads) & Smriti (Puranas & Ithihaasaas).

Rig Veda Shiva Sankalpa Suktam 18:

परात् परतरो ब्रह्मा तत्परात् परतो हरिः
तत्परात् परतोऽधीशस्तन्मे मनः शिवसङ्कल्पमस्तु

parAt parataro brahmA tatparAt parato hariH
tatparAt parato dhIshastanme manaH shivasaNkalpamastu

The greatest of the greatest is Brahma, but greater than him is Hari, but greater than Brahma & Hari is Shiva (also referred to as Mahadeva, Shambhu, Ishana, Ishvara). Let my mind focus on Shiva alone and not anyone else.

Katha Upanishad 2.1.13:

अङ्गुष्ठमात्रः पुरुषो ज्योतिरिवाधूमकः
ईशानो भूतभव्यस्य स एवाद्य स उ श्वः

aNguShThamAtraH puruSho jyotirivAdhUmakaH
IshAno bhUtabhavyasya sa evAdya sa u shvaH

The Purusha, of the size of a thumb, is like a flame without smoke and is the Lord of the past and the future. He exists as the same today and tomorrow (changeless).

Isha Upanishad Verse 1:

ॐ ईशा वास्यमिदꣳ सर्वं यत्किञ्च जगत्यां जगत् ।

AUM IshA vAsyamidagum sarvaM yatkincha jagatyAM jagat

Whatever exists in this changing universe animate or inanimate is under the control of Parama Shiva.

Rig Veda 10.90.2 & Shvetashvatara Upanishad 3.15 says: उतामृतत्वस्येशान

uta amRitatvasya ishAna

Lord Shiva is the Lord of Immortality

Mahadeva alone is described as the Lord of everything including the individual souls and the universe. Every individual soul has an eternal relationship with Lord Shiva alone. He is the dear friend of all the living entities and also the ultimate refuge for all.

Shvetashvatara Upanishad 3.17:

सर्वस्य प्रभुमीशानं **सर्वस्य शरणं सुहृत्** ॥

sarvasya prabhumIshAnaM **sarvasya sharaNaM suhRit**

Lord Shiva is the ultimate Lord of everything and the Supreme ruler of all. He is the **dear friend of all the living entities who resides in the heart and also the ultimate refuge for all**.

Hence Bhagavan Shiva alone is described as the essence of everything and the only object of surrender according to Sage Vishvaanara. Whatever the individual soul aspires for apart from Bhagavan Shiva, it is temporary and the individual soul would again float in the ocean of repeated birth and death.

Shvetashvatara Upanishad 3.8, 6.15:

तमेव विदित्वातिमृत्युमेति नान्यः पन्था विद्यतेऽयनाय

tameva viditvAtimRityumeti nAnyaH panthA vidyateyanAya

Only by knowing Bhagavan Shiva, one can transcend death. There is no other way to cross the repeated cycles of birth and death.

CHAPTER 5
Lord Shiva the Supreme Reality with divine qualities

VERSE 5:

शब्दं गृह्णास्यश्रवास्त्वं हि जिघ्रेरघ्राणस्त्वं व्यंघ्रिरायासि दूरात् ।
व्यक्षः पश्येस्त्वं रसज्ञोप्यजिह्वः कस्त्वां सम्यग्वेत्त्यतस्त्वां प्रपद्ये ।।

shabdaM griNhAsyashravAstvaM hi jighreraghrANastvaM vyamghrirAyAsi dUrAt |
vyakShaH pashyestvaM rasajnyopyajihvaH kastvAM samyagvetyatastvAM prapadye ||

Who can perfectly comprehend you O Lord Shiva? You are without ears yet you perceive sound; you are without a nose yet you smell; you are without foot yet you come from afar; you are without eyes yet you see everything; you are without tongue yet you can taste. Hence I resort only to you.

COMMENTARY:

Again this verse should be understood properly. Just because it is stated in this verse that Lord Shiva can see without eyes and hear without ears and taste without nose, walk without foot we cannot say that he is formless. As I have mentioned before, formlessness (**ananatatvam or infiniteness**) is an aspect of the formed Maheshvara. It is one of his attributes. Lord Shiva doesn't have eyes, nose, hands or feet like that of the individual soul's body. The individual soul's body is bound by birth, old age, disease, death, bound pleasure & pain, bound by virtues & sins, etc., whereas the **Supreme soul's form is divine, not bound by destruction, eternal, imperishable, free from sins, etc.** His features are described in the Vedas & Upanishads as the only object of meditation, devotion & surrender for attaining liberation.

Chandogya 8.7.1:

य आत्मापहतपाप्मा विजरो विमृत्युर्विशोको विजिघत्सोऽपिपासः सत्यकामः सत्यसंकल्पः सोऽन्वेष्टव्यः

ya AtmApahatapApmA vijaro vimRityurvishoko vijighatsopipAsaH satyakAmaH satyasaMkalpaH sonveShTavyaH

The Supreme soul is free from sins, old age, death, sorrow, without hunger and thirst, having true desires, he should be sought after to attain liberation.

The infiniteness of Lord Shiva is described in various places in the Upanishads & Puranas. But whenever Lord Shiva is described as without hands & without legs, AVYAKTAM, VIBHUM, ARUPAM it just talks about his all-pervasiveness. It doesn't mean that he doesn't have a form. Some people come to that wrong conclusion, but the divine attributes & characteristics of Lord Shiva are beautifully described in the Vedas, Upanishads, Puranas & Ithihaasaas (**Golden in complexion, eternally with Para Shakti, three-eyed, blue-necked, KrshnaPingala - dark and tawny (Ardhanaarishvara), five-faced, ten-handed, having the crescent moon on his head, having the skin of Narasimha (man-lion) & tiger for his garments, pure as crystal, one without a second, Pashupati - the Lord of all individual souls, Lord of five activities, the Supreme cause of all, one who doesn't have anyone to rule over him, etc.**). Lord Shiva is described as beyond all material forms.

We also saw the story where Vishnu acquired complete knowledge after meditating on the divine spiritual form of Lord Shiva within the infinite Jyoti (Refer to the commentary in the second verse).

Let's look at some of the references from the scriptures where Lord Shiva's all-pervasiveness is explained.

Shvetashvatara Upanishad 3.3 (The same verse is present in Maha Narayana Upanishad):

विश्वतश्चक्षुरुत विश्वतोमुखो विश्वतोबाहुरुत विश्वतस्पात् ।
सं बाहुभ्यां धमति सम्पतत्रैर्द्यावाभूमी जनयन् देव एकः ॥

vishvatashchakShuruta vishvatomukho vishvatobAhuruta vishvataspAt |
saM bAhubhyAM dhamati sampatatrair dyAvAbhUmI janayan deva ekaH ||

Lord Shiva's eyes are everywhere, faces everywhere, arms everywhere, everywhere are his feet. He brings together all the beings with his arms, encompasses them with his feet and having produced heaven and earth, he still remains as one without a second.

Shvetashvatara Upanishad 3.19 (The same verse is present in Kaivalya Upanishad 21, Mundaka Upanishad 1.1.6 & Suta Samhita Yajna Vaibhava Khanda Brahma Gita Chapter 7 Verse 6, Brahma Gita Chapter 8 Verse 49 with slight modifications):

अपाणिपादोजवनोग्रहीता पश्यत्यचक्षुः स शृणोत्यकर्णः ।
स वेत्ति वेद्यं न च तस्यास्ति वेत्ता तमाहुरग्र्यं पुरुषं महान्तम् ॥

apANipAdo javano grahItA pashyatyachakShuH sa shRiNotyakarNaH |
sa vetti vedyaM na cha tasyAsti vettA tamAhuragryaM puruShaM mahAntam ||

Lord Shiva can grasp everything without hands, hasting without feet, sees without eyes and hears without ears. He is the omniscient (knower of the past, present & future) but no one knows him. Lord Shiva is first & best of all, greater than the greatest & Ultimate Reality and complete in nature.

RUDRAM Anuvaaka 5 (Krishna Yajur Veda Taittiriya Samhita 4th Canto 5th Chapter), Shukla Yajur Veda Vaajasaneyi Samhita 16.30 glorifies Lord Shiva as: नमो अग्रियाय च प्रथमाय च

namo agriyAya cha prathamAya cha

Salutations to Lord Shiva who existed before creation and to him who is first among Gods.

Shvetashvatara Upanishad 3.10:

ततोयदुत्तरततं तदरूपमनामयम् ।
य एतद्विदुरमृतास्तेभवन्ति अथेतरेदुःखमेवापियन्ति ॥

tato yaduttaratataM tadarUpamanAmayam
ya etadviduramRitAste bhavanti athetare duHkhamevApiyanti

Lord Shiva is far beyond this world, is (**ARUPAM → BEYOND ALL MATERIAL FORMS**) and free from affliction. They who know him become immortal. All others indeed suffer pain alone.

Shvetashvatara Upanishad 3.11:

सर्वानन शिरोग्रीवः सर्वभूतगुहाशयः ।
सर्वव्यापी स भगवांस्तस्मात् सर्वगतः शिवः ॥

sarvAnana shirogrIvaH sarvabhUtaguhAshayaH
sarvavyApI sa bhagavAMstasmAt sarvagataH shivaH

Everywhere are his faces, heads, hands, necks. Lord Shiva dwells in the hearts of all beings. Lord Shiva is the all-pervading Bhagavan. He is the omnipresent and benevolent Lord.

Kurma Purana Canto 2 (Ishvara Gita) Chapter 2 Verses 46-49:

एष आत्माऽहमव्यक्तो मायावी परमेश्वरः ।
कीर्तितः सर्ववेदेषु सर्वात्मा सर्वतोमुखः ॥

सर्वकामः सर्वरसः सर्वगन्धोऽजरोऽमरः ।
सर्वतः पाणिपादोऽहमन्तर्यामी सनातनः ॥

अपाणिपादो जवनो ग्रहीता हृदि संस्थितः ।
अचक्षुरपि पश्यामि तथाऽकर्णः श्रृणोम्यहम् ॥

वेदाहं सर्वमेवेदं न मां जानाति कश्चन ।
प्राहुर्महान्तं पुरुषं मामेकं तत्त्वदर्शिनः ॥

esHa AtmA aham avyakto mAyAvI parameshvaraha
kIrtitah sarvavedesHu sarvAtmA sarvatomukhaha

sarvakamah sarvarasah sarvagandha ajarah amaraha
sarvatah pANipAda aham antaryAmI sanAtanaha

apANipAdo javano grahItA hrudi samsthitaha
achakshurapi pashyAmi tathAkarNah shrunomyaham

vedAham sarvamevedam na mAm jAnAti kaschana
prAhur mahAntam purusHam mAm ekam tattvadarshinaha

Lord Shiva says: I am the Supreme Soul, the master of Maya, the great Lord. I am glorified in the Vedas, as being the inner soul of all and having faces in all directions. I have within me all forms, tastes and fragrances. I am free from old age and death. I have hands and feet all around. I am the eternal immanent soul. Though handless and feetless I can grasp everything and am stationed in the heart of all. Though without eyes I observe everything and without ears, I can hear. I know all these. No one knows me. Persons of truthful vision call me as being the one and only great Purusha (Supreme Being).

Mundaka Upanishad 1.1.6 Sage Angiras says, Suta Samhita Brahma Gita 7.7 Sage Suta says:

नित्यं विभुं सर्वगतं सुसूक्ष्मं
तदव्ययं यद्भूतयोनिं परिपश्यन्ति धीराः

nityaM vibhuM sarvagataM susUkShmaM
tadavyayaM yadbhUtayoniM paripashyanti dhIrAH

The wise know Lord Shiva as eternal, omnipresent, all-pervading and extremely subtle who is imperishable and the source of all living beings.

Kaivalya Upanishad (The same verse is present with a slight modification in Suta Samhita Brahma Gita 8.10-11):

तमादिमध्यान्तविहीनमेकं विभुं चिदानन्दमरूपमद्भुतम्

tamAdimadhyAntavihInamekaM vibhuM chidAnandamarUpamadbhutam

Lord Shiva has no beginning, nor middle nor end; who is one and omnipresent; who is consciousness personified and full of Bliss; who is beyond all material forms and whose divine form is wonderful.

The Shruti (Vedas) always talks about the spiritual form of Bhagavan Shiva with divine attributes and at the same time it describes his omnipresence (or) infiniteness. The omnipresence cannot be claimed by individual souls (Jeevaatmaas) including devatas like Brahma, Hari, Lakshmi & Indra. Supporting this fact there is a beautiful verse in the Shiva Maha Purana.

Shiva Maha Purana Vidyeshvara Samhita Chapter 5 Verses 10-13, 15:

शिवैको ब्रह्मरूपत्वान्निष्कलः परिकीर्तितः
रूपित्वात्सकलस्तद्वत्तस्मात्सकलनिष्कलः

निष्कलत्वान्निराकारं लिंगं तस्य समागतम्
सकलत्वात्तथा बेरं साकारं तस्य संगतम्

सकलाकलरूपत्वाद्ब्रह्मशब्दाभिधः परः
अपि लिंगे च बेरे च नित्यमभ्यर्च्यते जनैः

अब्रह्मत्वात्तदन्येषां निष्कलत्वं न हि क्वचित्
जीवत्वं शंकरान्येषां ब्रह्मत्वं शंकरस्य च

Sage Suta said to the sages: Bhagavan Shiva alone is glorified as Nishkala (all-pervasive) and he is identified as the Supreme Brahman. He is also Sakala as he has a divine spiritual form. He is both Sakala and Nishkala. It is in his Nishkala (all-pervasive) aspect that the Linga is appropriate.

In the Sakala (divine spiritual form) aspect, the worship of his embodied form is appropriate. Since he has the Sakala and Nishkala aspects he is worshipped both in the Linga and in the divine spiritual form by the people and is called the Supreme Brahman. Other deities do not have the Nishkala aspect so they cannot be the Supreme Reality. Shankara is the only personality who can be regarded as the Supreme soul (Brahmatva) and all the others are all individual souls (Jeevatva).

As told here the omnipotence, omnipresence, etc. can be claimed only by Lord Shiva and not devatas like Brahma, Hari & Indra. He alone has the Nishkala (all-pervasiveness) aspect which is worshipped by everybody as the Linga. Because the Linga represents his infiniteness.

Shvetashvatara Upanishad 6.19:

निष्कलं निष्क्रियं शान्तं निरवद्यं निरञ्जनम्

niShkalaM niShkriyaM shAntaM niravadyaM niranjanam

The Supreme Lord Parama Shiva is Nishkala (all-pervasive), free from material actions, tranquil, faultless and spotless.

Brahma & Hari were fighting in EGO and Mahadeva appeared to destroy their ignorance and to give true knowledge to attain him appeared as an infinite column of fire with no beginning and end. That is the LINGA which represents his infiniteness.

But one will attain complete knowledge (PURNA JNYAANAM) by meditating on the form of Parama Shiva in the LINGA with the divine attributes and characteristics that he has been described in the Vedas, Upanishads & Puranas.

Rama inorder to cross the ocean and reach Lanka worshipped Lord Shiva. He glorifies Lord Shiva with beautiful verses and after worshipping him he has the divine vision of Para Shakti & Parama Shiva.

Padma Purana Paataala Khanda Chapter 116 Verses 222-225:

एवं स्तुवतो रामस्य पुरतो लिंगमध्यकोपेतस्तेजोमयमूर्तिराविर्बभूव अभयवानथ पुनः

पद्मासनासीनमुमाधिष्ठितांकमीशमामुक्तसर्वाभरणं सुकांतिकिरीटिनं हैमवतीकटिस्पर्शं

करद्वयेनाभयवरप्रदं तरंगितानेकदिशाभिः पूर्णतेजस्विनं हासमुखं प्रसन्नवदनं ददर्श

रामः परमेशितारं ननाम बद्धांजलिपुनश्च दंडवत्पपात अथ रामं परमेश्वरोऽपि

वरं वृणु त्वं वरदोऽहमित्युक्तवान्

In front of Rama who was praising Lord Shiva, an image full of luster appeared in the middle of the LINGA. He was granting fearlessness to Rama. Rama saw the Supreme Lord who had Parvathi on his lap, who had all ornaments on his body, whose crown was very bright, who was touching the waist of the daughter of the mountains, granting a boon of fearlessness, whose radiance was spread in all directions, whose had a smiling face. Rama with his palms joined saluted the Supreme Lord Shiva and fell prostrate before him like a staff. Then the Supreme Lord Shiva requests Rama to ask for boons.

Here the point to be noted is Para Shakti & Parama Shiva's divine form appeared in the middle of the LINGA.

This is how the Vedas, Upanishads, Puranas, etc. describe the infiniteness and all-pervasiveness of Saamba Shiva and then go on to describe his divine spiritual form and meditate on him to get relieved from the repeated cycles of birth and death.

The Maayaavaadis say the Supreme Reality is formless - NIRAAKAAR, without qualities - NIRGUNA. But Nirguna means one who is beyond the 3 modes (Sattva, Rajas, Tamas) of material nature. Formlessness is also described as an attribute of the Supreme Reality Bhagavan Shiva as we saw before. Mahadeva is Saguna Brahman (Supreme Lord with divine qualities) according to the Vedas, Upanishads & Puranas. One has to correlate all the Veda Vaakyams and then come to a conclusion and not see the scriptures in bits and pieces. Devotees of Lord Shiva who are inclined to Shiva Bhakti and who consider Shiva alone as the Supreme Reality should definitely stay away from these kinds of interpretations made by the Maayaavaadis.

A very similar verse as told by Sage Vishvaanara is spoken of in Isha Upanishad:

Isha Upanishad 5:

तदेजति तन्नैजति तद्दूरे तद्वन्तिके ।
तदन्तरस्य सर्वस्य तदु सर्वस्यास्य बाह्यतः ॥

tadejati tannaijati taddUre tadvantike
tadantarasya sarvasya tadu sarvasyAsya bAhyataH

Lord Shiva (The Ultimate Controller) moves and doesn't move. He is far away but at the same time, he is very near. He is within everything and also he is outside of everything.

This verse when looked at externally seems to exhibit the message that the Supreme Reality is formless. A lot of people come to that wrong conclusion, especially the Maayaavaadis. But the same Upanishad glorifies the divine form of Lord Shiva and goes on to say that the individual soul (Jeevaatmaa) should yearn for having the vision of the form of Lord Shiva which is the only pathway to liberation.

Isha Upanishad 15-16, Brihadaranyaka Upanishad 5.15.1:

हिरण्मयेन पात्रेण सत्यस्यापिहितं मुखम् ।
तत्त्वं पूषन्नपावृणु सत्यधर्माय दृष्टये ॥

hiraNmayena pAtreNa satyasyApihitaM mukham
tattvaM pUShannapAvRiNu satyadharmAya dRiShTaye

O Ultimate Supreme Reality (or) Ultimate Supreme Personality Saamba Shiva, your face is covered by your golden splendor. O Ultimate Protector, remove that and exhibit your divine spiritual form to me.

पूषन्नेकर्षे यम सूर्य प्राजापत्य व्यूह रश्मीन् समूह तेजः ।
यत्ते रूपं कल्याणतमं तत्ते पश्यामि योऽसावसौ पुरुषः सोऽहमस्मि ॥

pUShannekarShe yama sUrya prAjApatya vyUha rashmIn samUha tejaH
yatte rUpaM kalyANatamaM tatte pashyAmi yosAvasau puruShaH sohamasmi

O Saamba Shiva, you are the sole controller of the entire universe. Please withdraw your golden splendor. By your grace, I wish to see that divine spiritual form of yours that has divine qualities & attributes. I am the eternal servant of that Ultimate Purusha Lord Shiva.

As we have seen these 2 verses before, Lord Shiva's divine form should be meditated within the Linga which represents Mahadeva's all-pervasiveness. All the Upanishads do talk of Lord Shiva's all-pervasiveness and his divine attributes that should be meditated upon.

Taittiriya Upanishad:

स य एषोऽन्तहृदय आकाशः । तस्मिन्नयं पुरुषो मनोमयः । अमृतो हिरण्मयः ।

sa ya eSho antahRidaya AkAshaH tasminnayaM puruSho manomayaH amRito hiraNmayaH

In the space that is present in the heart, is this Supreme Person Parama Shiva who is realizable through knowledge and who is immortal and is golden.

Maha Narayana Upanishad:

य एषोऽन्तरादित्ये हिरण्मयः पुरुषः

ya eSho antarAditye hiraNmayaH puruShaH

He who is within the sun is the Golden Person

RUDRAM Anuvaaka 1 (Krishna Yajur Veda Taittiriya Samhita 4th Canto 5th Chapter), Shukla Yajur Veda Vaajasaneyi Samhita 16.6:

असौ यस्ताम्रो अरुण उत बभ्रुः सुमंगलः

asau yastAmro aruna utha babrusumangalaha

In the middle of the copper-red sun, Lord Shiva, the golden personality is present, who is all auspicious.

RUDRAM Anuvaaka 1 (Krishna Yajur Veda Taittiriya Samhita 4th Canto 5th Chapter), Shukla Yajur Veda Vaajasaneyi Samhita 16.7:

असौ योऽवसर्पति नीलग्रीवो विलोहितः

asau yo vasarpati nIlagrIvo vilohitaha

The blue-necked Lord Shiva rises in the copper-red colored sun.

Parashara Upa Purana Chapter 1 Verse 1:

सौरमण्डलमध्यस्थं साम्बं संसारभेषजम् ।
नीलग्रीवं विरूपाक्षं नमामि शिवमव्ययम् ॥ १ ॥

saura mandala madhyastham sAmbam samsArabheshajam
nIlagrIvam virUpAksham namAmi shivam avyayam

I offer my humble prostrations to the Supreme Lord Parama Shiva who dwells in the middle of the sun along with mother Para Shakti. He is the ultimate lord who is blue-necked, odd-eyed (three-eyed), all auspicious, imperishable and releases the individual souls from the repeated cycles of birth and death.

Kurma Purana Canto 1 Chapter 15 Verse 15: Sage Dadichi says to Daksha:

एष रुद्रो महादेवः कपर्दो च घृणी हरः ।
आदित्यो भगवान् सूर्यो नीलग्रीवो विलोहितः ।।

He is Rudra, the Supreme God Mahadeva, compassionate & shining with great splendor, Hara, the personality who is present as the inner soul of SUN, blue-necked & ruddy.

All the scriptures related to Surya like Saura Samhita of Skanda Purana, Aditya Upa Purana and Saura Upa Purana glorify only Mahadeva and always talk of meditating Lord Shiva along with Amba in the middle of the sun.

His divine form alone is Shuddha Sattva (pure mode of goodness) and his form alone is the object of meditation, object of worship and object of surrender according to the Vedas, Upanishads, Puranas, etc. and he alone is regarded as the creator of Brahma, Narayana, Kaala Rudra & Indra.

So in this verse, Sage Vishvaanara describes the all-pervasive nature of Lord Shiva who is described to have a divine form that is indestructible and residing in the heart of all the living entities present as the true witness. Only by acquiring unflinching faith, devotion to that Supreme Lord Shiva, meditating on his divine form in the heart, singing his praises & glories and surrendering to him one can achieve the highest peace (PARAMA SHAANTI).

CHAPTER 6
Only a true devotee can understand Lord Shiva

VERSE 6:

नो वेदस्त्वामीश साक्षाद्विवेद नो वा विष्णुर्नो विधाताऽखिलस्य ।
नो योगींद्रा नेंद्रमुख्याश्च देवा भक्तो वेद त्वामतस्त्वां प्रपद्ये ।।

no vedastvAmIsha sAkShAdviveda no vA viShNur no vidhAtAKhilasya |
no yogIndrA nendramuKyAshca devA bhakto veda tvAmatastvAM prapadye ||

The Vedas cannot comprehend you directly, O Lord Shiva, neither Vishnu, nor Brahma, nor the leading Yogis, nor the Devas including Indra can understand you. Only a true devotee can comprehend you. Hence I surrender to you alone.

COMMENTARY:

Sage Vishvaanara is right in saying that the Vedas, Brahma, Vishnu, Indra and the Yogis cannot understand Lord Shiva. We can see some references for this statement in various places of the scriptures told by Hari, Brahma, Vyasa, etc.

Narada Purana Purva Bhaga Chapter 79 Verses 137-139 (The same is present in Padma Purana Paataala Khanda Chapter 114 Verses 185-190):

श्रुतिदेवाद्यगम्यं हि पदं तव कपिस्थितम् ।
सर्वोपनिषदव्यक्तं त्वत्पदं कपिसर्वयुक् ।।

यमादिसाधनैर्योगैर्न क्षणं ते पदं स्थिरम् ।
महायोगिहृदंभोजे परं स्वस्थं हनूमति ।।

वर्षकोटिसहस्रं तु सहस्राब्दैरथान्वहम् ।
भक्त्या संपूजितोऽपीश पादो नो दर्शितस्त्वया ।।

shrutidevAddhyagamyam hi padam tava kapisthitam
sarvopanisHadavyaktam tvatpadam kapisarvayuk

yamAdisAdhanair yogair na kshanam te padam sthiram
mahAyogi hrudambhoje param svastham hanUmati

varsHakotisahasram tu sahasrAbdair athAnvaham
bhaktyA sampUjitopIsha pAdo no darshitastvayA

Hari says to Lord Shiva: The Vedas are still searching for your feet. Your feet which the monkey (Hanuman) has attained are still being searched by all the Upanisads. Your feet are not attained by means of restraining one's senses and deep meditation and it has not been manifested in the lotus of the heart of sages who have been practicing penance and meditating on your feet for crores of years; but how lucky Hanuman is, who is holding your feet. For crores of years, I devoutly worshipped and searched the feet of yours, O Supreme Lord, but you did not manifest it to me.

NOTE: Here Hari says that even the Vedas, Upanishads and the divine sages including himself are trying to worship and search for his feet but they haven't seen them even after meditating for crores of years. But Hanuman has acquired that chance of holding the feet of Lord Shiva. Hanuman is described as a great devotee of Lord Shiva. We also know of the famous story where Brahma was searching for the head of Lord Shiva and Vishnu was searching for the feet of Lord Shiva and they failed to attain success in their search. Finally, Lord Shiva manifests himself to them and blesses them. Here Vishnu (or) Hari concedes to that truth by saying that he is still searching for the feet of Lord Shiva and is unable to find them.

FEET OF LORD SHIVA; VISHNU WORSHIPPING PARVATHI & LORD SHIVA

Padma Purana Paataala Khanda Chapter 105 Verse 234, Brihat Jabala 6th Brahmana 10th Verse:

न शक्तिं भस्मनो जाने प्रभावं वा कुतस्तव
नमस्तेऽस्तु नमस्तेऽस्तु त्वामेव शरणं गतः

na shaktiM bhasmano jAne prabhAvam vA kuthasthava
namastestu namastestu tvAmeva sharaNam gataH

Hari says to Bhagavan Shiva: I cannot understand the power of the sacred ash, when can I understand your glories O Mahadeva? Salutation to you, salutation to you. I seek your refuge alone.

Mahabharata Drona Parva Chapter 202 Verses 109-111: Sage Vyasa says to Arjuna:

वेदाः साङ्गोपनिषदः पुराणाध्यात्मनिश्चयाः ।
यदत्र परमं गुह्यं स वै देवो महेश्वरः ।।

ईदृशश्च महादेवो भूयांश्च भगवानजः ।
न हि सर्वे मया शक्या वक्तुं भगवतो गुणाः ।।

अपि वर्षसहस्रेण सततं पाण्डुनन्दन ।

vedAh sAngopanishadah purAnAdhyAtma nishchayAha
yadatra paramam guhyam sa vai devo maheshvaraha

Idhrushashcha mahAdevo bhUyAmscha bhagavAn ajaha
na hi sarve mayA shakyA vakthum bhagavatho gunAha

api varsha sahasreNa sathatham pAndunandhana

Whatever is highly mysterious in the several branches of the Vedas, Upanishads, Puranas, and in those sciences whatever deals with talking about the Supreme Soul is attributed to the Supreme Lord Maheswara. Mahadeva that only God without birth. All the attributes of that Supreme God (bhagavAn) Shiva cannot be mentioned by me even if I were to recite them continuously for a thousand years, O son of Pandu.

Skanda Maha Purana Kaashi Khanda Uttaraardha Chapter 95 Verse 60:

यं वै वेदो वेद नो नैव विष्णुर्नोवा वेधा नो मनो नैव वाणी ।
तं देवेशं मादृशः कोल्पमेधा याथात्म्याद्वै वेत्त्यहो विश्वनाथम् ।।

yam vai vedo veda no naiva vishNurnAvA vedhA no mano naiva vANI
tam devesham mAdrushah kolpamedhA yAthAtmyAdvai vethyaho vishvanAtham

Sage Vyasa says to Bhagavan Shiva: Which man of meager intellect like me can understand you, O Vishvanatha? Even the Vedas, Brahma, Hari, mind, or speech cannot understand you who is the Lord of the Universe and Lord of the Devas.

Skanda Purana Arunaachala Mahatmya Uttaraardha Chapter 16 Verses 1-5:

ब्रह्मोवाच
देवदेव तवैश्वर्यं केन शक्येत वेदितुम् ।
विना भायैक्यसुलभं भवदीयमनुग्रहम् ।।

अकर्तृकाणि वाक्यानि ऐश्वर्यं ते निरत्ययम् ।
न स्तोतुं शक्यते किं तु नमस्कुर्वंति दूरतः ।।

को विष्णुः कोऽहमेते वा दिक्पाला वासवादयः ।
त्वमेव देव कर्त्तासि जगत्सृजनरक्षयोः ।।

पतिस्त्वं पार्वतीनाथ पशवो वयमप्यमी ।
बद्धं पाशेन मोक्तुं वा त्वमेवास्मान्प्रगल्भसे ।।

षड्विंशत्तत्त्वरूपस्त्वमभितश्चाभिवर्त्तसे ।
कोविदः को विनिर्णेतुं तव याथात्म्यमीश्वरः ।।

Brahma says to Lord Shiva: O Lord of the Devas, by whom can you glory and power be comprehended without your blessing which can be acquired by your grace. Words have no makers. Your supreme glories are faultless. It is not possible to eulogize you. Who is Vishnu? Who am I? Who are these Guardians of the Quarters beginning with Indra? You alone, O Lord, are the cause of creation and preservation of the entire universe. O Lord of Parvathi, you are Pathi (the ultimate Lord). All of us (including Brahma & Hari) are Pashu (individual souls). You alone are competent to bind us with Paahsa (noose) and can also liberate us from bondage. You are of the nature of the twenty-six principles. You pervade all. O Ishvara, who is intelligent enough to understand your true nature.

Brahma Vaivarta Purana Krishna Janma Khanda Chapter 36 Verse 106, 108:

तस्यायुषः प्रमाणं च नाहं जानामि का श्रुतिः।।
शंकरः परमात्मा मे प्राणेभ्योऽपि परः शिवः।।
त्र्यम्बके मन्मनः शश्वन्न प्रियो मे भवात्परः ।।

tasuAyusHah pramANam cha nAham jAnAmi kA shrutihi
shankarah paramAtmA me prANebhyopi parah shivaha
tryambake manmanah shashvan na priyo me bhavAtparaha

Krishna says to Radha: I am not aware of Lord Shiva's age and even the Vedas (Shruti) don't know his age. Shiva is the Supreme Lord and my inner soul (Supreme soul → antarAtmA) who is greater than my own life. I always devote my mind to Tryambaka (three-eyed Lord Shiva). No one is greater than Lord Shiva.

There is a place in the Puranas where the sages come to test mother Parvathi and ask her why is she attracted to Lord Shiva and why can't she marry someone else; to which mother Parvathi replies to the sages:

Padma Purana Srishti Khanda Chapter 43 Verses 335-340, Matsya Purana Chapter 154 Verses 345-351:

प्रजापतिसमाः सर्वे भवंतः सर्वदर्शिनः
न नूनं वित्थ तं देवं शाश्वतं जगतः प्रभुम्

अजमीशानमव्यक्तममेयमहिमोदयम्
आस्तां तत्कर्मसद्भावं संबोधं तावदावृतम्

विदुस्तं न हरि ब्रह्ममुखा अपि सुरेश्वराः
यत्तस्यविभवं स्वोत्थं भुवनेषु विजृंभितम्

प्रकटं सर्वभूतानां तदप्यथ न वित्थ किं
कस्यैतद्गगनं मूर्तिः कस्याग्निः कस्य मारुतः

कस्य भूः कस्य वरुणः कश्चंद्रार्कविलोचनः
कस्यार्चयंति लोकेषु लिंगं भक्त्या सुरासुराः

यच्च ब्रह्मेश्वरा देवा विष्ण्विन्द्राद्या महर्षयः
प्रभावं प्रभवं वापि तेषामपि न वित्थ किं

All of you sages are omniscient. Yet you do not know that Supreme Lord Parama Shiva, who is eternal and the only lord of the universe, who is unborn, who is the ultimate ruler, who is immutable and whose greatness and glories are immeasurable. Even the devatas like Hari and Brahma cannot understand him, who is the ultimate reality and object of all knowledge. Do you not even know that greatness of him, which has spread in all the worlds and is clear to all beings, whose manifestations are earth, water, fire, air and ether, whose eyes are the moon and the sun, whose Linga is devoutly worshipped by the demons and devatas led by Brahma, Hari, Indra and the sages? Do you not even know Lord Shiva who is the source of their power?

Brahmanda Purana Purva Bhaga Anushanga Chapter 26:

This chapter deals with the story of Brahma and Hari fighting with each other on supremacy. Lord Shiva appears as an infinite column of fire to crush their ego. This story is shared to other devatas by Vishnu when they question the glory of Lord Shiva. I am sharing some verses where they express their inability to locate the ends of Lord Shiva and finally surrender to him.

Verses 27-30:

ततो वर्षसहस्रं तु ह्यहं पुनरधो गतः ।।
न पश्यामि च तस्यांतं भीतश्चाहं ततोऽभवम् ।।

तथैव ब्रह्मा ह्यूध्व च न चांतं तस्य लब्धवान् ।।
समागतो मया सार्द्ध तत्रैव च महाभसि ।।

ततो विस्मयमापन्नौ भीतौ तस्य महात्मनः ।।
मायया मोहितौ तेन नष्टसंज्ञै व्यवस्थितौ ।।

ततो ध्यानरतौ तत्र चेश्वरं सर्वतोमुखम् ।।
प्रभवं निधनं चैव लौकानां प्रभुमव्ययम् ।।

Hari says to the Devatas: I went far below for a thousand years but I could not find the end. I became frightened thereby. Similarly, Brahma went upwards, but he too did not reach its extremity. He too returned along with me to that vast expanse of water. We were surprised and frightened of the Supreme soul. We were deluded by the Maya Shakti of the Supreme Reality Bhagavan Shiva. Our consciousness got lost and we stayed there helplessly. Therefore, we meditated upon the Supreme Lord Mahadeva with faces on all sides, the imperishable lord who is the cause of all causes and the cause of the dissolution of all the worlds (Paataala Loka till Vishnu Loka).

NOTE: This story of Brahma and Hari searching for Lord Shiva is present in various Puranas: Shiva, Linga, Skanda, Padma, Brahmanda, Vayu, Kurma, Parashara, Aditya, Narada, Devi Bhagavata, Brahma, Agni, etc.

Pancha Brama Upanishad Verses 18, 19:

आदावन्ते च मध्ये च भाससे नान्यहेतुना ।
मायया मोहिताः शम्भोर्महादेवं जगद्गुरुम् ॥

न जानन्ति सुराः सर्वे सर्वकारणकारणम् ।
न सन्दृशे तिष्ठति रूपमस्य परात्परं पुरुषं विश्वधाम ॥

AdAvante cha madhye cha bhAsase nAnyahetunA

mAyayA mohitAH shambhormahAdevam jagadgurum

na jAnanti surAH sarve sarvakAraNakAraNam
na sandRushe tiShThati rUpamasya parAtparaM puruSham vishvadhAma

Bewildered by the Maya Shakti of Shambhu, the devatas do not understand him; who is the Guru and Lord of the universe and the cause of all the causes. His form cannot be seen with material eyes who is the highest of the highest and the support of the universe and by whom the universe is manifested.

We have various references like this in the scriptures talking about the incapability of Brahma and Hari in understanding the Supreme Lord Shiva. Even the Vedas & Upanishads cannot understand Lord Shiva. So who can understand Lord Shiva?

Only a devotee can understand Lord Shiva. Some of the qualities of a devotee of Lord Shiva are:

1) Hearing the glories of Lord Shiva from the scriptures from authentic Vaidika Shaiva Gurus
2) Chanting Panchaakshaara Mantra (NAMAH SHIVAAYA) and doing Shiva Naama Sankirtanam
3) Wearing the Tripundra, Bhasma, Rudraaksha
4) Worshipping the Linga & Vigraha of Lord Shiva
5) Not engaging in the worship of devatas like Hari, Brahma, Indra, Lakshmi, etc.
6) Singing songs praising Lord Shiva
7) Having unflinching faith that Lord Shiva alone is the Supreme Lord
8) Spending time with Shiva Bhaktas and serving them
9) Meditating on the divine form of Lord Shiva in the heart
10) Eating Saatvic (vegetarian) food
11) Feeling compassionate for other souls

12) Engaging in selfless devotional service to Lord Shiva, not aspiring for anything material and not being interested in the positions of Hari, Brahma, Lakshmi & Indra.

13) Spreading the knowledge of Lord Shiva to other individual souls

These are some of the qualities spoken in the Upanishads, Puranas & Agamas. By performing these one can easily attain Saamipya (nearness) to Lord Shiva.

THIS PICTURE DEPICTS THE RESULT OF SELFLESS DEVOTIONAL SERVICE TO MAHADEVA

Let us see some examples of devotees from the scriptures who attained Lord Shiva.

Varaha Purana Chapter 213: The Greatness of Gokarneshvara: Verses 55-59:

न प्रभुत्वं न देवत्वं नेन्द्रत्वमपि वा प्रभो ।।
ब्रह्मत्वं लोकपालत्वं नापवर्गं वरप्रद ।।

नैवाष्टगुणमैश्वर्यं गाणपत्यं न च प्रभो ।।
स्पृहये देवदेवेश प्रसन्ने त्वयि शंकर ।।

यदि प्रीतोऽसि भगवन्ननुक्रोशतया मम ।।
अनुग्राह्यो ह्ययं देव त्वयावश्यं सुराधिप ।।

यथान्ये न भवेद्भक्तिस्त्वत्तो नित्यं महेश्वर ।।
तथाहं भक्तिमिच्छामि सर्वभूताशये त्वयि ।।

यथा च न भवेद्विघ्नं तपस्यानिरतस्य मे ।।

Sage Nandi says to Lord Shiva: I don't desire lordship, the status of devatas, Indra, Brahma or Vishnu, liberation or eight-fold power or leadership of Ganas. O Supreme Lord Shankara if you are pleased with me and wish to favor me, ***please give me that kind of devotion that will make me worship you alone and none else***. I wish to have devotion for you who resides in the heart of all the living entities & devatas. Let there be no impediment to this.

This should be the attitude of a devotee. A devotee of Lord Shiva is not interested in anything. He or she is not interested in acquiring the positions of Brahma, Hari, Lakshmi, Indra, etc. because a devotee knows that even these positions are also temporary. The only thing that a devotee aspires for, is to engage in selfless devotional service to Lord Shiva eternally. Here we see the example of Nandi where he asks Lord Shiva for a boon where he would worship him alone and none else and let there not be any impediments in his worship of

Lord Shiva. This is true devotion. Only for a devotee of this kind, Lord Shiva would reveal himself. After this, Lord Shiva becomes really satisfied and gives Saarupya (his form) to Nandi and makes him his eternal servant.

Varaha Purana Chapter 213 Verses 68, 69:

मद्रूपधारी मत्तेजास्त्र्यक्षः सर्वगुणोत्तमः ।।
भविष्यसि न सन्देहो देवदानवपूजितः ।।

अनेनैव शरीरेण जरामरणवर्जितः ।।
दुष्प्राप्येयमवाप्ता ते देवैर्गाणेश्वरी गतिः ।।

You will get a form and splendor like mine, three-eyed and endowed with all virtues and worshipped by Devas and Asuras. With this body which will be free from age and death, you will also be the leader of the Shiva Ganaas.

Narada Purana Uttara Bhaga Chapter 72: The Power of Austerities of Gautama: Verses 19-22:

ततस्तत्तपसा तुष्टो भगवानंबिकापतिः ।।
सगणो दर्शनं यातो वरं ब्रूहीत्युवाच ह ।।

Lord Shiva (Ambika Pathi → Husband of Ambika) became delighted with the penance of Sage Gautama and appeared before him along with his Ganaas and said: "Tell me, what is the boon you would choose to have?"

ततो मुनिवरो दृष्ट्वा देवदेवमुमापतिम् ।।
त्र्यंबकं स नमश्चक्रे निपत्य भुवि तत्पुरः ।।

On seeing Lord Shiva (Uma Pathi → Husband of Uma) who is three-eyed and the lord of all devatas, the excellent sage fell on the ground in front of him and made obeisance.

तत उत्थाय सहसा कृतांजलिरुपस्थितः ।।
प्रोवाच देहि मे भक्तिं पादयोस्तव नित्यदा ।।

Rising up immediately, he joined his palms in reverence and prayed to Lord Shiva: ***Grant me devotion unto your feet forever***.

Narada Purana Uttara Bhaga Chapter 73: The Greatness of Tryambakeshvara: Verse 117:

आगच्छतानादि मुमुक्षवो ये यूयं शिवं चिंतयतांतरेऽब्जे ।।
ध्यायंति मुक्त्यर्थममुं हि नित्यं वेदांतविज्ञानसुनिश्चितार्थाः ।।

Sage Jaimini says: O individual souls who are seeking liberation, come and think of Lord Shiva within your lotus heart. Indeed those persons who have decisively learned the perfect Vedaantic knowledge, perpetually meditate on Mahadeva for the sake of salvation.

After reciting the wonderful **Veda Paada** hymn which consists of 113 verses, Sage Jaimini was blessed by Bhagavan Shiva and attains Ganaadhipatyam (the post of leader of Ganaas in Maha Kailasha).

Mahabharata Anushaasana Parva Chapter 14 Verse 352:

यदि देयो वरो मह्यं यदि तुष्टोऽसि मे प्रभो।
भक्तिर्भक्तु मे नित्यं त्वयि देव सुरेश्वर।।

Sage Upamanyu says to Lord Shiva: If, O Lord, you are pleased with me and if you would grant me boons, let this be the boon, O Lord of all the devatas: ***My devotion to you may remain perpetual & unflinching***.

Skanda Purana Avanti Khanda Avanti Ksetra Mahatmya Chapter 38 Verses 27-30:

यच्च ते मनसा वापि किंचिच्च कांक्षितं फलम् ।।
तत्तत्सर्वं प्रदास्यामि ब्रूहि दानवसत्तम ।।

Lord Shiva said to Andhaka: Tell me whatever that you have desired in your mind. I shall grant you.

ब्राह्म्यं वैष्णवमेंद्रं वा पदमावृत्तिलक्षणम् ।।
विदितं मम तत्सर्वं मनागपि न कांक्षये ।।

यदि तुष्टोऽसि देवेश गाणपत्यं ददस्व मे ।।
सविशेषं विशुद्धं च तदक्षय्यं च सर्वदा ।।

Andhaka said to Lord Shiva: ***The positions of Brahma, Hari & Indra are characterized by coming and going. All this is known to me. I do not desire them at all.*** O Lord of devatas, if you are pleased, please grant me Gaanapathya (leader of the Shiva Ganaas), which is something that is pure and perpetual (everlasting).

अमरो जरया त्यक्तः सर्वदुःखविवर्जितः ।।
भविष्यसि गणाध्यक्षः सर्वलोकनमस्कृतः ।।

Lord Shiva said to Andhaka: You shall become the presiding officer of the Ganaas (devotees of Bhagavan Shiva in Maha Kailasha), devoid of death, without old age and all kinds of miseries. You shall be bowed down to by the entire world.

Skanda Purana Kaashi Khanda Chapter 95 Verse 63:

नान्यं देवं वेद्म्यहं श्रीमहेशान्नान्यं देवं स्तौमि शंभोर्ऋतेऽहम् ।।
नान्यं देवं वा नमामि त्रिनेत्रात्सत्यं सत्यं सत्यमेतन्मृषा न ।।

Sage Vyasa ends his octet to Bhagavan Shiva by saying: I do not know any other Lord than Maheshvara; I do not eulogize another Lord except Shambhu; I do not bow down to a Lord other than the Three-eyed One. This is the truth, the truth, the truth, not a lie.

Vayu Purana Puurvaardha Chapter 55 Verse 60, Brahmanda Purana Purva Bhaga Anushanga Chapter 26 Verse 60:

यदि प्रीतिः समुत्पन्ना यदि देयो वरश्च नौ ।
भक्तिर्भवतु नौ नित्यं त्वयि देव सुरेश्वर ।।

Brahma and Hari said to Lord Shiva: O lord of the devatas, if you are delighted and if a boon has to be bestowed by you, ***let us always be devoted to you forever***.

Padma Purana Paataala Khanda Chapter 105 Verses 236-237:

त्वत्पादयुगले शंभो भक्तिरस्तु सदा मम
अथ दत्वा वरं शंभुरिदमाह वचो हरिम्
भस्मधारणसंपन्नो मम भक्तो भविष्यसि

Hari said to Lord Shiva: ***O Shambhu, let me always have devotion to your feet***. Then having granted the boon Shambhu said to Vishnu: "By applying the sacred ash (Bhasma or Vibhuti), you will be my devotee."

Padma Purana Paataala Khanda Chapter 117 Verses 182-186:

वरं वृणु प्रसन्नोऽस्मि ब्रह्मादेरपि दुर्लभम्
तवादेयं न मे किंचिद्वृणु त्वं न चिराय वै

Bhagavan Shiva says to Rama: I am pleased with you, ask for a boon which is difficult to be had even by Brahma and others.

न याच्यं मे जगन्नाथ भूराज्यं मम सांप्रतम्
स्वर्गश्च कर्म्मभिः प्राप्तो भक्तिस्त्वत्पाददर्शनात्

आरोग्यं पश्य भुंजेऽहं सा सीता योषितां वरा
वशीकृताः सर्वनृपाः प्रजाधर्मसमन्विताः

हर्ष एव ममापन्नस्त्वदागमनतोऽच्युत
तथापि वरये किंचिद्भक्तिरस्तु स्थिरा त्वयि

Rama said to Bhagavan Shiva: O lord of all the worlds, I have nothing to ask for. By your grace now I have the entire kingdom in my possession. I have devotion through seeing your feet. I have good health and Sita is my wife. I have subjugated all the kings. My subjects are endowed with righteousness. O imperishable Supreme soul, I have become glad by your arrival. Yet I shall ask for something. ***Let my devotion to you be stable always.***

Skanda Purana Kaashi Khanda Chapter 26 Verses 58-60:

यदि प्रसन्नो देवेश देवदेव महेश्वर
भवान्या सहितं त्वां तु द्रष्टुमिच्छामि सर्वदा

सर्वकर्मसु सर्वत्र त्वामेव शशिशेखर
पुरश्चरं तं पश्यामि यथा तन्मे वरस्तथा

त्वदीय चरणांभोज मकरंदमधूत्सुकः
मच्चेतो भ्रमरो भ्रांतिं विहायास्तु सुनिश्चलः

Vishnu says to Lord Shiva: O Lord of the devatas, O Supreme Lord Maheshvara, if you are pleased, I wish to always see you in the company of Bhavani (Parvathi). The boon to be granted to me, O moon-crested Lord is such as should enable me to see you going ahead everywhere at the time of all my activities***. Let my mind that resembles a black bee cease to wander and be enthusiastic for the honey issuing from the lotus-like feet of yours.*** Let it be always steady.

We saw examples of great personalities & sages like Nandi, Upamanyu, Bhringi, Gautama, Jaimini, Vyasa, etc. All of them asked only for one thing: "**I am not interested in the positions of Brahma, Hari & Indra. Let my devotion to your feet be stable**". Even devatas like Brahma & Hari are also devoted to Lord Shiva and ask for the same. A true devotee of Lord Shiva is not interested in acquiring the positions of Brahma, Vishnu & Indra which are temporary. He or she would always hanker to engage in eternal service to Lord Shiva & Shiva Ganaas.

That's why here Sage Vishvaanara says no one including the Vedas, Upanishads, Brahma, Vishnu, Indra & meditating sages can understand Bhagavan Shiva but only a BHAKTA (devotee) who is engaged in selfless devotional service can understand & attain Bhagavan Shiva.

CHAPTER 7
Lord Shiva the UNBORN

VERSE 7:

नो ते गोत्रं नेश जन्मापि नाख्या नो वा रूपं नैव शीलं न देशः ।
इत्थंभूतोपीश्वरस्त्वं त्रिलोक्याः सर्वान्कामान्पूरयेस्तद्भजे त्वाम् ।।

no te gotraM nesha janmApi nAKyA no vA rUpaM naiva shIlaM na deshaH |
itthaMbhUtopIshvarastvaM trilokyA sarvAnkAmAn pUrayestadbhaje tvAm ||

O Ishvara, you don't have a lineage (GOTRA), you are unborn, you are immortal, beyond all material forms and not bound by the modes of material nature (SATTVA, RAJAS, TAMAS). Still, you are the lord of all the worlds and fulfill all our desires. Hence I resort to you and worship you alone.

COMMENTARY:

This is a very interesting verse as it talks about the various unique qualities of Bhagavan Shiva. Every Purana talks about the marriage of mother Parvathi & Parameshvara who are the parents of the entire universe including devatas like Brahma, Hari & Indra. One should always meditate on the divine pastimes of Lord Shiva; the foremost being his marriage with mother Parvathi. All of the living beings including the divine sages and devatas like Brahma, Hari, Indra & Lakshmi wanted to participate and see the marriage of Parvathi & Parameshvara. When Bhagavan Shiva comes to the place of Himavan, there is a beautiful conversation that happens between Himavan and Lord Shiva.

Vamana Purana Canto 1 Chapter 27 Verses 41-44:

सुखासीनास्य शर्वस्य कृताञ्जलिपुटो गिरिः।
प्रोवाच वचनं श्रीमान् धर्मसाधनमात्मनः।।

To Sharva who was comfortably seated, the great Himavan with folded hands spoke words leading to virtue and merit.

हिमवानुवाच
मत्पुत्रीं भगवन् कालीं पौत्रीं च पुलहाग्रजे।
पितृणामपि दौहित्रीं प्रतीच्छेमां मयोद्यताम्।।

Himavan said to Lord Shiva: Please accept my daughter, granddaughter of the elder brother of Pulaha and the daughter of the daughter of Pitrs, offered by me.

NOTE: Here we should not be confused thinking that mother Parvathi has a human birth. She is eternal like Parama Shiva. She appears by her own will in the house of Himavan to bless the devotees, for the welfare of the world and to spread Shiva Bhakti. One should never compare the appearance of mother Parvathi with that of incarnations of Vishnu like Rama, Krishna, etc. Hari had to take birth on account of curses and not out of his own will. Vishnu and incarnations of Vishnu including Rama, Krishna are bound by birth, old age, disease & death.

इत्येवमुक्त्वा शैलेन्द्रो हस्तं हस्तेन योजयन्।
प्रादात् प्रतीच्छ भगवन् इदमुच्चैरुदीरयन्।।

Saying this and putting away the palm of the bride on that of the groom the lord of the mountains gave his daughter in marriage, saying "O Lord, please accept her."

हर उवाच
न मेऽस्ति माता न पिता तथैव न ज्ञातयो वाऽपि च बान्धवाश्च।
निराश्रयोऽहं गिरिश्रृङ्गवासी सुतां प्रतीच्छासि तवाद्रिराज।।

Lord Shiva said to Himavan: I have no mother, no father and similarly no maternal or paternal relations. I am alone and am present at the peak of the mountains. O King of mountains, I accept your daughter.

MARRIAGE OF MOTHER PARVATHI AND PARAMESHVARA

Here Bhagavan Shiva himself reveals his true nature that he is unborn and doesn't have a mother or father. This has also been mentioned in many places by Sage Narada, Brahma, Vishnu, Vyasa, etc. Mahadeva is also described in the same way in the Vedas & Upanishads (**ajAyamAno badhudhA vijAyathe**).

इत्येवमुक्त्वा वरदोऽवपीडयत् करं करेणाद्रिकुमारिकायाः।
सा चापि संस्पर्शमवाप्य शंभोः परां मुदं लब्धवती सुरर्षे।।

Saying this much the Boon giving Shambhu held the hand of the daughter of Himavan with his own hand. Mother Parvathi getting the contact with Mahadeva experienced great pleasure.

Skanda Purana Maheshvara Khanda Kedhaara Khanda Chapter 25 Verses 76-83:

अस्य गोत्रं कुलं नाम न जानंति हि पर्वत॥
ब्रह्मादयो हि विवुधा अन्येषां चैव का कथा॥

त्वं हि मूढत्वमापन्नो न जानासि हि किंचन॥
वाच्यावाच्यं महेशस्य विषया हि बहिर्मुखाः॥

येये आगमिकाश्चाद्रे नष्टास्ते नात्र संशयः॥
अरूपोयं विरूपाक्षो ह्यकुलीनोऽयमुच्यते॥

अगोत्रोऽयं गिरिश्रेष्ठ जामाता ते न संशयः॥

Sage Narada says to Himavan: O Parvatha (Mountain), devatas beginning with Brahma, Vishnu & Indra do not know his Gotra (lineage); what to speak of others? You are confounded. You do not know anything about what should be or should not be said. All worldly objects are external to Maheshvara. O Mountain, whatever is originated, whatever has birth, becomes dead. There is no doubt about it. This Virupaksha (the one with odd eyes is beyond all material forms (He is Shuddha

Sattva). Hence he is called Akulina (one who doesn't have a GOTRA). O excellent Himavan, your son-in-law is undoubtedly one without a Gotra.

ब्रह्मापि तं न जानाति मस्तकं परमेष्ठिनः॥
विष्णुर्गतो हि पातालं न दृष्टो हि तथैव च॥

तेन लिंगेन महता ह्यगाधेन जगत्त्रयम्॥
व्याप्तमस्तीति तद्विद्धि किमनेन प्रयोजनम्॥

अनयाराधितं नूनं तव पुत्र्या हिमालय॥
तत्त्वतो हि न जानासि कथं चैव महागिरे॥

Brahma cannot understand him as he failed to find Lord Shiva's head. Vishnu went to the nether worlds searching for Lord Shiva's feet and he failed. The whole range of the three worlds has been pervaded by that unfathomable Linga. Understand this. That Linga has been worshipped by your daughter. The entire universe is created and sustained by Para Shakti & Parama Shiva.

There is a place where Daksha out of arrogance scolds Bhagavan Shiva but that becomes a song of praise.

Skanda Maha Purana Kaashi Khanda Uttaraardha Chapter 87 Verse 28:

किं वंश्यस्त्वेष किं गोत्रः किं देशीयः किमात्मकः
किं वृत्तिः किं समाचारो विषादी वृषवाहनः

Daksha says: Does he come under anyone's control? What is his Gotra? What is his native land? What is his nature? What is his job of sustenance? What is his conduct of life? He eats poison. His vehicle is a bull.

Let's decode this verse sung by Daksha to Lord Shiva:

Does he come under anyone's control?

Mahadeva is not under the control of anybody. Everything is under his control. He is the Lord of everything including Brahma, Narayana, Kaala Rudra & Indra.

Atharvashikha Upanishad:

परमात्मनि सम्प्रतिष्ठाप्य ध्यायीतेशानं प्रध्यायितव्यं सर्वमिदं ब्रह्मविष्णुरुद्रेन्द्रास्ते

सम्प्रसूयन्ते सर्वाणि चेन्द्रियाणि सह भूतैर्न कारणं कारणानां ध्याता कारणं तु ध्येयः

सर्वैश्वर्यसम्पन्नः शंभुराकाशमध्ये ध्रुवं स्तब्ध्वाधिकं शिव एको ध्येयः शिवंकरः

सर्वमन्यत्परित्यज्य समस्ताथर्वशिखैतामधीत्य द्विजो गर्भवासाद्विमुक्तो विमुच्यत

एतामधीत्य द्विजो गर्भवासाद्विमुक्तो विमुच्यत इत्योꣳसत्यमित्युपनिषत्

paramAtmani sampratiShThApya dhyAyIteshAnaM pradhyAyitavyam sarvamidaM brahmaviShNurudrendrAste

samprasUyante sarvANi chendriyANi saha bhUtairna kAraNam kAraNAnAm dhyAtA kAraNam tu dhyeyaH

sarvaishvaryasampannaH shaMbhurAkAshamadhye dhruvam stabdhvAdhikam shiva eko dhyeyaH shivamkaraH

sarvamanyatparityajya samastAtharvashikhaitAmadhItya dvijo garbhavAsAdvimukto vimuchyata

etAmadhItya dvijo garbhavAsAdvimukto vimuchyata ity om satyam ityupaniShat

Brahma, Vishnu, Rudra and Indra and all the senses with their respective elements, originate from Him. The cause of all causes Ishana alone should be meditated upon. He alone is the object of meditation. Shambhu who is the Lord of all, the Supreme soul and endowed with all perfections like Omnipotence, Omniscience, Omnificence, prosperity, etc. is to be meditated in the middle of the ether of the heart (daharAkAsha). Lord Shiva alone is to be meditated upon, who is the doer of good casting aside everything. Thus, concludes the Atharvashikha. The twice-born one, who studies this Upanishad attains liberation and never enters a mother's womb. Thus ends the Upanishad.

What is his Gotra? What is his native land?

No one is aware of Lord Shiva's lineage. He doesn't belong to a lineage as he doesn't have birth and he doesn't belong to any nationality. Crores and crores of universes are under his control. He alone is described as birthless. Everybody including Brahma, Vishnu & Indra are bound by birth, old age, disease & death.

अजायमानो बहुधा विजायते

ajAyamAno bahuthA vijAyate

Although He is unborn, the inner-self of all, he manifests himself as the manifold universe.

Padma Purana Paataala Khanda Chapter 108 Verses 69-70:

ब्रह्माधिकबलो विष्णुरायुषि ब्रह्मणोऽधिकः
ब्रह्मांडमालाभरणे महेशस्य ममैव तु
चतुर्निःश्वासमात्रेण विष्णोरायुरुदाहृतम्

Saamba Shiva said: Vishnu has more power than Brahma and has also longer life than Brahma. But the life of Vishnu is said to be of the measure of four inhalings of Maheshvara and me.

So by this, we come to know that everybody including Brahma and Hari are bound by birth, old age, disease and death. Bhagavan Shiva alone is beyond birth and death. That's why there is no lineage (GOTRA) for Bhagavan Shiva.

What is his nature?

His real nature is that he is eternal, indestructible, infinite and the ultimate ruler.

Shvetashvatara Upanishad 6.7:

तमीश्वराणां परमं महेश्वरं तं देवतानां परमं च दैवतम् ।
पतिं पतीनां परमं परस्ताद्- विदाम देवं भुवनेशमीड्यम् ॥

tamIshvarANAM paramaM maheshvaraM taM devatAnAM paramaM cha daivatam
patiM patInAM paramaM parastAdh vidAma devaM bhuvaneshamIDyam

Bhagavan Shiva is the Supreme Lord of lords, the Supreme Deity of deities, the Ruler of all rulers; who is higher than the Prakriti and is the self-luminous, adorable Lord of the world.

Keeping this in mind, even in Harivamsha Purana, Lord Shiva is glorified as the **ultimate ruler (sarveshvareshvaram)**.

Harivamsha 2-74-19:

उदकं च गृहायाथ बिल्वं च हरिरव्ययः ।
देवमावाहयामास रुद्रं सर्वेश्वरेश्वरम् ।।

udakaM cha gRihAyAtha bilvaM cha hariravyayaH |
devamAvAhayAmAsa rudraM **sarveshvareshvaram** ||

Hari (Vishnu) took water and bilva leaves and invoked the **Supreme Lord Rudra, the Lord of all devatas**.

What is his job of sustenance? What is his conduct of life?

He is described as the doer of five activities (creation, maintenance, destruction, concealment and liberation). Though Brahma and Hari are described as creators and protectors respectively. They are creators and protectors only in the secondary sense. Lord Shiva alone is the primary creator and protector. He sustains the entire universe including all the individual souls starting from the blade of grass to Vishnu.

Rig Veda 9.96.5, Sama Veda Puurvaarchikaa Chapter 5 Sloka 527, Sama Veda Uttaraarchikaa Chapter 5 Sloka 943:

सोमः पवते जनिता मतीनां जनिता दिवो जनिता पर्थिव्याः |
जनिताग्नेर्जनिता सूर्यस्य जनितेन्द्रस्य जनितोत विष्णोः ||

Para Shakti & Parama Shiva (Shiva + Uma → SOMA, RUDRAM 8th Anuvaaka: namah somAya cha) glorified by holy hymns who begot Earth, Heaven, Agni, Surya, Indra & Vishnu.

Pancha Brahma Upanishad:

पञ्चकृत्यनियन्तारं पञ्चब्रह्मात्मकं बृहत् ।
पञ्चब्रह्मोपसंहारं कृत्वा स्वात्मनि संस्थितः ॥

panchakRityaniyantAraM panchabrahmAtmakaM bRihat
panchabrahmopasamhAram kRitvA svAtmani samsthitaha

He is the cause of the five activities in the form of the five (Sadyojaataa, Vaamadeva, Aghora, Tatpurusha, Ishaana). He alone remains at the time of final dissolution absorbing all the manifestations into himself.

He eats poison. His vehicle is a bull.

Daksha says he ate poison. Lord Shiva drank the poison and kept it in his throat to save the entire universe. No one including Brahma and Hari was capable of drinking the poison. The terrible Halaahala poison destroyed the entire universe including Brahma Loka and Vaikuntha. Hari turned black on account of that poison.

Skanda Purana Maheshvara Khanda Kedhaara Khanda Chapter 9 Verse 109:

तावत्प्रवृद्धं सुमहत्कालकूटं समभ्ययात्॥
दग्ध्वादो ब्रह्मणो लोकं वैकुण्ठं च ददाह वै॥

The great poison Kaalakuta came there. After burning Brahma's world, it also burned Vaikuntha (Vishnu's world).

Vayu Purana Canto 1 Chapter 54 Verse 58, Brahmanda Purana Anushanga Chapter 25 Verse 57:

निर्दग्धो रक्तगौरांगो कृतः कृष्णो जनार्द्दनः ।।

Janardhana (Vishnu) of reddish-white body had turned black on being scorched by the Kaalakuta poison.

Matsya Purana Chapter 250 Verse 46:

विष्णुः कृष्णः कृतस्तेन यमश्च विषमात्मवान्।
मूर्च्छिताः पतिताश्चान्ये विप्रनाशङ्गताः परे ।।

Devatas say to Lord Shiva: The Kaalakuta poison is very powerful on account of which Vishnu has turned black, dismayed Dharmaraja, rendered many unconscious and killed several.

The Vedas & Upanishads highlight these names: Neelagriva (six times in RUDRAM), Neelakantha (two times → Kaivalya and Shiva Sankalpa), Shitikantha (three times in RUDRAM) when talking about the Supreme Reality. Also, it shows how compassionate Lord Shiva is towards all the devatas, asuras and the universe.

RUDRAM Anuvaaka 5 (Krishna Yajur Veda Taittiriya Samhita 4th Canto 5th Chapter), Shukla Yajur Veda Vaajasaneyi Samhita 16.28:

नमो नीलग्रीवाय च शितिकण्ठाय च

namo nIlagrIvAya cha shitikaNThAya cha

Salutations to him who has a blue neck and who has a dark-blue throat.

The bull represents DHARMA (righteousness) and righteousness is the vehicle or is under the control of Lord Shiva.

Saura Upa Purana Chapter 45 Sloka 58, Linga Purana Canto 2 Chapter 18 Sloka 38:

सत्यं ब्रह्म महादेवं पुरुषं कृष्णपिंगलम् ।।
ऊर्ध्वरतेसमीशानं विरूपाक्षमजोद्भवम् ।।

satyam brahma mahAdeva purusHam krushNapingalam
urdhvaretasam IshAnam virUpAksham ajodbhavam

He is the personification of righteousness and truth. He is the Supreme Brahman. He is dark and tawny-colored (Uma Maheshvara). He is Supreme of all, odd-eyed (three-eyed). He is Ishana (ultimate ruler), birthless and the ultimate cause of everything.

Shadaksharam Stotram Verse 5:

वाहनं वृषभो यस्य वासुकिः कंठभूषणम् ।
वामे शक्तिधरं देवं वकाराय नमो नमः ॥

vAhanam vrshabho yasya vAsukih Kanttha bhUshanam |
vAme shakti dharam devam vakArAya namo namaha ||

Salutations to him who has a Bull (NANDI) as his vehicle, who has the snake Vaasuki as an ornament on his neck, who has the divine Mother Shakti on his left. Salutations to that Lord Shiva, Who is represented by the syllable "Vaa", The fifth syllable of the Shadakshara mantra "Om-Na-Ma-Shi-Vaa-Ya".

Mahadeva is Dharmeshvara or the Lord of Righteousness. Though Daksha recites the verse to insult Lord Shiva but actually if we analyze it properly, it’s a beautiful song of praise.

When mother Parvathi appeared in the house of Himavan and Menavathi, sage Narada made a visit to have a glimpse of mother Parvathi. At that time, when Himavan and Menavathi enquire about Parvathi to sage Narada, Narada makes some statements by which Himavan was taken aback. Sage Narada then decodes the statements he made in detail to give a proper understanding to Himavan. We are going to see one of them.

Matsya Purana Chapter 154 Verse 145: न जातोऽस्याः पति (na jAtosyAha pati)

Sage Narada says to Himavan and Menavathi: Her husband is not yet born.

Matsya Purana Chapter 154 Verses 167, 168:

त्वया चोक्तं हि देवर्षे! न जातोऽस्याः पतिः किल ।
एतद्दौर्भाग्यमतुलमसंख्यं गुरु दुःसहम् ।।

चराचरे भूतसर्गे यदद्यापि च नो मुने ।
न स जात इति ब्रूषे तेन मे व्याकुलं मनः ।।

Himavan says to Sage Narada: O Sage, You have said that her husband is not yet born which is a most unlucky and unbearable thing. You have also said that her Lord is not born in the universe of the three worlds which has caused great agitation in my mind.

Matsya Purana Chapter 154 Verses 176-185:

स्मितपूर्वमुवाचेदं नारदो देवचोदितः।
हर्षस्थानेऽपि महति त्वया दुःखं निरूप्यते ।।

अपरिच्छिन्नवाक्यार्थे मोहं यासि महागिरे!।
इमां श्रृणु गिरं मत्तो रहस्यापरिनिष्ठताम् ।।

समाहितो महाशैल! मयोक्तस्य विचारणे।
न जातोऽस्याः पतिर्देव्या यन्मयोक्तं महाबल! ।।

न स जातो महादेव भूतभव्य भवोद्भवः।
शरण्यः शाश्वत शास्ता शङ्करः परमेश्वरः ।।

ब्रह्मविष्णिवन्द्रमुनयो जन्ममृत्युजरार्दिताः।
तस्यैते परमेशस्य सर्वे क्रीड़नका गिरे! ।।

आस्ते ब्रह्मा तदिच्छातः संभूतो भुवनप्रभुः।
विष्णुर्युगे युगे जातो नानाजातिर्महातनुः ।।

मन्यसे मायया जातं विष्णुञ्चापि युगे युगे।
आत्मनो न विनाशोऽस्ति स्थावरान्तेऽपि भूधर!।।

संसारे जायमानस्य म्रियमाणस्य देहिनः।
नश्यते देह एवात्र नात्मनो नाश उच्यते।।

ब्रह्मादिस्थावरान्तोऽयं संसारो यः प्रकीर्त्तितः।
स जन्ममृत्युदुःखार्त्तो ह्यवशः परिवर्त्तते ।।

महादेवोऽचलः स्थाणर्न जातो जनकोऽजरः।
भविष्यति पतिः सोऽस्या जगन्नाथो निरामयः ।।

Sage Narada says to Himavan: You are driven to anxiety even in the midst of good fortunes and all good luck. O mighty mountain, You have been deluded because you have not interpreted my words correctly. Now hear the hidden truth from me. Be careful in deciphering what I have said. Her Lord is not a born one. Because Mahadeva the Eternal Lord, Protector of the Past, Present and Future is never born. He alone is the refuge of all, the Immutable and devatas like Brahma, Hari & Indra and the Sages are all subject to the cycle of birth, death and old age. They are instruments in the hands of Mahadeva. It is through the wish of Mahadeva that Brahma is the Lord of Brahma Loka and Vishnu manifests himself in various ways taking different bodies during different Yugas by Lord Shiva's grace. Vishnu & incarnations of Vishnu are temporary and bound to destruction (bound by Maheshvara Maya). Lord Shiva who is the Paramatma (Supreme soul) is not bound by death. Starting from Brahma, Vishnu down towards the blade of grass and immovable objects like trees are subject to the pangs of birth & death. Mahadeva alone is free from disease and death, fixed, immovable and is never born. He is not subject to old age and is free from all diseases. From him sprang everything. Such Mahadeva who is the Lord of the universe will be the husband of your daughter.

So we can understand that Mahadeva alone is described as birthless and deathless. Only a birthless personality can give the state of immortality and not someone who is bound by birth and death.

Some fools say that Rudra appeared from the forehead of Brahma or Narayana and denigrate Lord Shiva by saying he has a cause. The personality that comes from the forehead of Brahma or Narayana is Kaala Rudra and not Parama Shiva.

Parama Shiva & Kaala Rudra are differentiated in the Vedas, Upanishads, Puranas, Upa-Puranas, Smritis, Ithihaaasaas, etc. Parama Shiva has always been declared as the cause of Brahma, Narayana & Kaala Rudra.

We already saw a reference from Padma Purana at the beginning where Brahma & Narayana originate from the right and left limbs of Lord Shiva and Kaala Rudra originates from the heart of Parama Shiva. Let's see some more references.

Kurma Purana Canto 1 Chapter 26 Verses 88, 89:

पश्येतं मां महादेवं भयं सर्वं प्रमुच्यताम् ।
युवां प्रसूतौ गात्रेभ्यो मम पूर्वं सनातनौ ।।

अयं मे दक्षिणे पार्श्वे ब्रह्मा लोकपितामहः ।
वामपार्श्वे च मे विष्णुः पालको हृदये हरः ।।

Lord Shiva says to Brahma & Hari: Have a look at me the Supreme God Mahadeva; may all your fears be eschewed. Formerly, both of you, the eternal ones, were born of my limbs. Brahma, the grandfather of the world is on my right side; Hari the protector of the world is on my left side and Hara (Kaala Rudra) resides in my heart.

Mahabharata Anushaasana Parva Chapter 14 Verses 347-348:

योऽसृजद्दक्षिणादङ्गाद्ब्रह्माणां लोकसम्भवम्।
वामपार्श्वात्तथा विष्णुं लोकरक्षार्थमीश्वरः।।

युगान्ते चैव सम्प्राप्ते रुद्रमीशोऽसृजत्प्रभुः।
स रुद्रः संहरन्कृत्स्नं जगत्स्थावरजङ्गमम्।।

Upamanyu says to Lord Shiva: You created Brahma from your right limb and Vishnu from your left limb. You created Kaala Rudra during the end of the Yuga when the entire creation needs to be dissolved. That Kaala Rudra who sprang from you destroys the entire creation with all its mobile and immobile beings.

Brahmanda Purana Purva Bhaga Anushanga Chapter 26 Verse 58, Vayu Purana Puurvaardha Chapter 55 Verse 58:

अयं मे दक्षिणो बाहुर्ब्रह्मा लोकपितामहः।
वामो बाहुश्च मे विष्णुर्नित्यं युद्धेषु तिष्ठति।

Lord Shiva says: Brahma is my right hand. Vishnu is my left hand.

Brihat Jabala Upanishad:

त्रिनेत्रं त्रिगुणाधारं त्रयाणां जनकं प्रभुम्
स्मरन्नमः शिवायेति ललाटे तत्त्रिपुण्ड्रकम्

trinetram triguNAdhAram trayANAm janakaM prabhum
smarannamaH shivAyeti lalATe tattripuNDrakam

One should draw the Tripundra (Bhasma or Vibhuti) on the forehead meditating on Lord Shiva who has the three eyes, who is beyond the three modes of material nature (Sattva, Rajas, Tamas) and who is the father of the three (Brahma, Narayana, Kaala Rudra) while reciting the mantra "NAMAH SHIVAAYA".

Everywhere he is described as beyond the three modes of material nature (Sattva, Rajas, Tamas) and the creator of Brahma, Narayana & Kaala Rudra.

It is out of the wish of Lord Shiva that his partial manifestation Kaala Rudra appears from the forehead of Brahma or Narayana to help both of them in the creation and maintenance of the universe. Hence RUDRAM glorifies Lord Shiva as: नमो अग्रियाय च प्रथमाय च

namo agriyAya cha prathamAya cha

Salutations to him who existed before creation and to him who is the first among everything.

नमः पूर्वजाय चापरजाय च नमो मध्यमाय च

namaH pUrvajAya chAparajAya cha namo madhyamAya cha

Salutations to him who was present before everybody and to him who appears after the creation and during the middle of the creation.

Kurma Purana Canto 1 Chapter 10 Verse 17:

कच्चिन्न विस्मृतो देवः शूलपाणिः सनातनः ।
यदुक्तवानात्मनोऽसौ पुत्रत्वे तव शंकरः ।।

Vishnu says to Brahma: Have you forgotten that you requested the trident-bearing eternal Lord Mahadeva to be your son?

Kurma Purana Canto 1 Chapter 26 Verses 97-98:

भविष्यत्येव भगवांस्तव पुत्रः सनातनः
अहं च भवतो वक्त्रात् कल्पादौ सुररूपधृक्
शूलपाणिर्भविष्यामि क्रोधजस्तव पुत्रकः

Lord Shiva says to Hari: I, the eternal Lord will appear with a trident in my hand as your son by coming out of your mouth at the beginning of a Kalpa.

So there are many more references like this that Lord Shiva is the creator of Brahma, Narayana & Kaala Rudra and he is beyond the trinity. The difference between Kaala Rudra and Parama Shiva is stated unanimously in Vedas, Puranas, Upa-Puranas, Smritis, Ithihaasaas, etc.

So Lord Shiva alone is birthless and **ayonija → not born from a womb**.
Next, he is described as beyond the three modes of material nature. Everywhere in the Upanishads & Puranas Lord Shiva is described as Shuddha Sattva (beyond Sattva, Rajas, Tamas). His form is also not touched by the three modes of material nature.

Kaivalya 4, Mundaka 3.2.6, Maha Narayana 12.15 Upanishads:

परेण नाकं निहितं गुहायां विभ्राजते यद्यतयो विशन्ति
वेदान्तविज्ञानसुनिश्चितार्थाः संन्यासयोगाद्यतयः शुद्धसत्त्वाः ।
ते ब्रह्मलोकेषु परान्तकाले परामृताः परिमुच्यन्ति सर्वे ॥

pareNa nAkaM nihitaM guhAyAM vibhrAjate yadyatayo vishanti
vedAntavijnAnasunishrchitArthAH sanyAsayogAdyatayaH shuddhasattvAH
te brahmalokeShu parAntakAle parAmRitAH parimuchyanti sarve

Lord Shiva is dwelling in the cave of the heart and is radiant. The Yatis attain him who are possessed of a firm conviction resulting from the knowledge of the Vedanta (Upanishads → End of the Vedas) and whose minds are purified by renouncing worldly desires. All of them at the end of their life go to the highest world (Maha Kailasha) of Brahman (Supreme Reality → Parama Shiva) and get liberated from the repeated cycles of birth and death and become immortal.

Shiva Gita Chapter 14 Verse 37:

दैवी ह्येषा गुणमयी मम माया दुरत्यया ।
मामेव ये प्रपद्यन्ते मायामेतां तरन्ति ते ॥

daivI hyeshA guNamayI mama mAyA duratyayA
mAm eva ye prapadyante mAyAm etAm taranti te

Lord Shiva says to Rama: This Maayaa Shakti consisting of three qualities Sattva, Rajas and Tamas is very difficult to overcome by anyone. Only those who surrender to me can easily cross it.

NOTE: This verse also comes in Bhagavad Gita 7.14. As we have seen before in the commentary to the second verse, Bhagavad Gita was spoken by Lord Shiva and Bhagavad Gita is verily the form of Lord Shiva. It was given to Arjuna by Lord Shiva using Krishna as an instrument.

So all these references clearly declare that he is not touched by the material modes of nature and he is beyond the three modes (SHUDDHA SATTVA).

He is also described as the lord of all the worlds right from Paataala Loka including Indra, Brahma, Vaikuntha, Goloka, Skanda and Devi lokas.

RIG 5.3.3:

तव श्रिये मरुतो मर्जयन्त रुद्र यत ते जनिम चारु चित्रम |
पदं यद विष्णोर उपमं निधायि तेन पासि गुह्यं नाम गोनाम ||

tava shriye maruto marjayanta rudra yat te janima cAru citram |
padam yad vishnor upamam nidhAyi tena pAsi ghuhyam nAma ghonAm ||

O Rudra the one with great splendor, Vishnu acquired the position of being the Lord of Vaikuntha along with Lakshmi by worshipping you in the Shiva Linga.

Always the Veda Mantras & Upanishads should be understood with the help of a supporting fact (Upa-Brihmanam). Let's see the supporting facts for this Veda Mantra.

Parashara Upa Purana Chapter 16 Verse 15-19:

ददाति सर्वजन्तूनामचिरादेव सत्तम ।
रौद्रं लिङ्गं महाविष्णुर्भक्त्या शुद्धं शिलामयम् ।। १५ ।।
चारुचित्रं समभ्यर्च्य लब्धवान्[2] परमं पदम् ।
या[3] च लक्ष्मीः समाख्याता महाविष्णोश्च वल्लभा ।। १६ ।।
यस्य लिङ्गं समभ्यर्च्य संपूज्यः सर्वचेतनैः ।

Vishnu acquired the position of being the protector of the universe and also acquired Vaikuntha along with Lakshmi as his wife by worshipping the Mahadeva in the Shiva Linga who is with great splendor and who is the cause of all individual souls. (Note the word **chAruchitram** which also comes in the RIG Mantra).

ब्रह्मा सर्वजगत्कर्ता यस्य लिङ्गार्चनेन तु ।। १७ ।।
भारतीं प्राप्तवानाशु, स पूज्यः सर्वचेतनैः ।
यस्य[4] लिङ्गं समभ्यर्च्य स्वभर्तुर्वल्लभाऽभवत् ।। १८ ।।
शची देवी स्त्रियश्चान्याः स पूज्यः सर्वचेतनैः ।
यस्य लिङ्गं समभ्यर्च्य मरुतः सकला अपि ।। १९ ।।

Brahma acquired the position of being the creator of the universe and acquired Sarasvathi as his wife by worshipping the Mahadeva in the Shiva Linga who is with great splendor and who is the cause of all individual souls. Indra acquired the position of being the in charge of heaven (Svarga) and acquired Shachi as his wife by worshipping the Mahadeva in the Shiva Linga who is with great splendor and who is the cause of all individual souls. The same worship was done by Maruts and all other devatas and they acquired their positions respectively.

Skanda Purana Kaashi Khanda Chapter 23 Verse 65:

वैकुंठैश्वर्यमासाद्य हरेरित्थं हरः स्वयम् ।।
कैलासे प्रमथैः सार्धं स्वैरं क्रीडत्युमापतिः ।।

Lord Shiva the consort of Uma, granting Vaikuntha and the entire Aishwarya (prosperity) to Hari, always freely sports about in Kailasha along with Mother Parvathi and the Pramatha Ganaas (devotees of Lord Shiva).

From this, we can understand that Vishnu acquired the position of being in charge of Vaikuntha, Goloka by engaging in Shiva Puja. The same with Brahma, Indra and all other devatas. Lord Shiva alone is the lord of all the worlds.

Shvetashvatara Upanishad 3.17:

सर्वस्य प्रभुमीशानं सर्वस्य शरणं सुहृत् ॥

sarvasya prabhumIshAnaM sarvasya sharaNaM suhRit

Lord Shiva is the ultimate Lord of everything and the Supreme ruler of all. He is the dear friend of all the living entities who resides in the heart and also the ultimate refuge for all.

As a dear friend, he fulfills the desire of all the living entities and also the devatas. He also punishes them if they are bound by EGO. So casting aside everything one should resort to Lord Shiva alone who is the doer of good to everybody. He is described as **sarvAnkAmAnpUraya** by Sage Vishvaanara which means he fulfills all the desires of all the living entities. There is nothing wrong in worshipping Bhagavan Shiva having material desires in mind. But in course of time, the worship of Bhagavan Shiva with sakAma (with desires) should become nishkAma (without desires). Because, at the end of the day whatever we desire apart from Bhagavan Shiva, it is temporary. Lord Shiva alone is the Supreme Reality immutable, indestructible.

CHAPTER 8
Lord Shiva the Lord of all including Brahma & Hari

VERSE 8:

त्वत्तः सर्वं त्वं हि सर्वं स्मरारे त्वं गौरीशस्त्वं च नग्नोऽतिशांतः ।
त्वं वै वृद्धस्त्वं युवा त्वं च बालस्तत्त्वं यत्किंनास्यतस्त्वां नतोस्मि ।।

tvattaH sarvaM tvaM hi sarvaM smarAre tvaM gaurIshastvaM cha nagnotishAntaH |
tvaM vai vriddhastvaM yuvA tvaM cha bAlastatvaM yatkiM nAsyatastvAM natosmi ||

Everything originates from you, O enemy of Kaama (Smara); you are the lord of everything. You are the Lord of mother Gauri; you are without clothes and highly quiescent. You are aged, you are the youth and child. What is it that is not related to you? Hence I bow down and surrender only to you.

COMMENTARY:

We have already seen various references in the commentary to the second verse (**Sage Vishvaanara says: ekah kartA**) where Lord Shiva is described as the cause of all causes and the ultimate cause from whom everything including Brahma, Hari, Indra, Earth, etc. originates. Let us see some more references.

Mahabharata Drona Parva Chapter 202 Verses 12-14:

महादेवं हरं स्थाणुं वरदं भुवनेश्वरम् ।
जगत्प्रधानमजितं जगत्प्रीतिमधीश्वरम् ।।

जगद्योनिं जगद्बीजं जयिनं जगतो गतिम् ।
विश्वात्मानं विश्वसृजं विश्वमूर्तिं यशस्विनम् ।।

विश्वेश्वरं विश्वनरं कर्मणामीश्वरं प्रभुम् ।
शंभुं स्वयंभुं भूतेशं भूतभव्यभवोद्भवम् ।।

mahAdevam haram sthANum varadam bhuvaneshvaram
jagatpradhAnam ajitam jagatprItim adhIshvaram

jagatyonim jagatbIjam jayinam jagato gatim
vishvAtmAnam vishvasrujam vishvamUrtim yashasvinam

vishveshvaram vishvanaram karmaNAm Ishvaram prabhum
shambhum svayambhum bhUtesham bhUtabhavyabhavodbhavam

Sage Vyasa says to Arjuna: The Supreme Deity and boon-giving lord of the universe is referred to as Mahadeva, Hara and Sthanu. He is the foremost of every being in the universe, he is incapable of being vanquished, he is the delighter of the universe and its supreme ruler. The ultimate cause of everything, the light and refuge of the universe and he is ever victorious. He is the soul and the creator of the universe and also having the universe for his form, he is the giver of prosperity (aishwarya) to all the devatas and all the living entities. He is the lord of the universe and rules over it; he is the master of all actions. Also called Shambhu, he is self-born (not created by anybody), he is the lord of all creatures and the origin of the past, present and future.

Atharvashiras Upanishad:

अहमेकः प्रथममासं वर्तामि च भविश्यामि च नान्यः कश्चिन्मत्तो व्यतिरिक्त इति

ahamekaH prathamamAsaM vartAmi cha bhavishyAmi cha nAnyaH
kashchinmatto vyatirikta iti

When the devatas asked the question “who are you” to Lord Shiva, Lord Shiva replied to the devatas: “I alone was present in the beginning before creation and even prior to beginningless time, I am present now and I will be present in the future. There is nothing that exists apart from me, the Supreme Lord".

Shvetashvatara Upanishad 6.9:

स कारणं करणाधिपाधिपो न चास्य कश्चिज्जनिता न चाधिपः

sa kAraNaM karaNAdhipAdhipo na chAsya kashchijjanitA na chAdhipaH

He is **the ultimate cause of all** and the ruler of individual souls. **He is without a progenitor or controller**.

Shvetashvatara Upanishad 6.13:

नित्यो नित्यानां चेतनश्चेतनानामेको बहूनां यो विदधाति कामान् ।
तत्कारणं साङ्ख्ययोगाधिगम्यं ज्ञात्वा देवं मुच्यते सर्वपाशैः ॥

nityo nityAnAM chetanashchetanAnAm eko bahUnAM yo vidadhAti kAmAn
tatkAraNaM sANkhyayogAdhigamyaM jnAtvA devaM muchyate sarvapAshaiH

He is the Eternal among the eternal, the intelligent among all that is intelligent. Though one without a second he fulfills the desires of everyone. One is released from all bondage on realizing Lord Shiva, the self-luminous lord, the ultimate cause who can be understood by knowledge and devotion.

Mahadeva is described as the enemy of Kaama deva as he burnt Kaama into ashes. Hence he is called Kaameshvara. Kaama and Kaala are always under the control of Lord Shiva.

Indra was attracted to the beauty of Sage Gautama's wife Ahalya, on account of which he was cursed by Sage Gautama. Moon (Chandra) was attracted to the wife of Sage Brihaspati. Sage Vishvamitra was attracted to a celestial woman named Menaka. Sages Vyasa & Bharadvaja were attracted to the beauty of a celestial woman named Ghritachi. Everybody including the devatas like Brahma and Hari were bound by lust.

Inorder to destroy the EGO of Brahma, Kaala Bhairava, the partial manifestation of Lord Shiva cut the fifth head of Brahma with the tip of his nail.

NOTE: Kaala Bhairava and Veerabhadra are partial manifestations of Lord Shiva and not Lord Shiva themselves. Some people misunderstand that Kaala Bhairava & Veerabhadra are Lord Shiva themselves. They are great devotees of Lord Shiva and they engage in fulfilling the wish of Lord Shiva. Even Brahma & Hari cannot withstand Kaala Bhairava & Veerabhadra who are just partial manifestations of Lord Shiva then what to speak of Lord Shiva himself.

Some fools say that Kaala Bhairava was bound by Brahma Hatya. But people don't realize that it is under the order of Lord Shiva, Kaala Bhairava does the rite of expiation to show an example to the world and not because he was bound by Brahma Hatya.

Shiva Maha Purana ShataRudra Samhita Chapter 8 Verse 62:

ब्रह्महत्यापनोदाय व्रतं लोकाय दर्शय

Lord Shiva says to Kaala Bhairava: Show the world the rite of expiation for removing the sin of slaying a brahmin.

Shiva Maha Purana ShataRudra Samhita Chapter 9 Verses 31, 32:

संहारकाले संप्राप्ते सदेवान्निखिलान्मुनीन् ।।
लोकान्वर्णाश्रमवतो हरिष्यसि यदा हर ।।

तदा कृते महादेव पापं ब्रह्मवधादिकम् ।।
पारतन्त्र्यं न ते शम्भो स्वैरं क्रीडत्यतो भवान् ।।

When Kaala Bhairava goes to Vaikuntha to bless Vishnu & Lakshmi, Vishnu glorifies Kaala Bhairava as follows: When the time of dissolution comes, O destroyer of the world, you annihilate all the devatas, sages and people of all castes and stages of life. Then, the sin of slaying brahmins and others does not affect you. You are not bound by these and are quite independent. You sport as you please.

Shiva Maha Purana ShataRudra Samhita Chapter 9 Verses 36, 40:

यश्चिन्तयति पुण्यात्मा तव पादाम्बुजद्वयम् ।।
ब्रह्महत्याकृतमपि पापन्तस्य व्रजेत्क्षयम् ।।

अद्य मे परमो लाभस्त्वद्य मे मंगलं परम् ।।
तं दृष्ट्वामृत तृप्तस्य तृणं स्वर्गापवर्गकम् ।।

If a pious soul contemplates on the lotus-like pair of your feet, even his sin of brahmin-slaughter comes to an end. I have the greatest of gains today. I have the most auspicious of signs today. Even this Vaikuntha and liberation are as insignificant as a blade of grass to me who am contented with the nectar of seeing you.

Kaala Bhairava destroys everything including the devatas, sages & people at the time of dissolution. So Vishnu clearly says when Kaala Bhairava destroys everything at the end of time how the sin of slaying a brahmin can affect him. Also, he goes on to say that the sin of killing a brahmin perishes by meditating on Kaala Bhairava's feet. He also yearns to have the vision of Kaala Bhairava. These are just glorifications of a devotee of Lord Shiva → Kaala Bhairava. So what to speak of Lord Shiva himself. A devotee of Lord Shiva (liberated soul) himself can remove the sins of the fallen individual souls like Brahma & Hari too. So it doesn't make sense when people try to ridicule saying Kaala Bhairava was bound by Brahma Hatya.

Lord Shiva is described in RUDRAM as beyond sins & virtues:

या ते रुद्र शिवा तनू-रघोराऽपापकाशिनी

yA te rudra shivA tanUraghorA **apApakAshinI**

O Lord Shiva, one who showers happiness by dwelling in the Mount with your aspect which is peaceful and the giver of good always and that which is **beyond sins and virtues**.

Mahadeva alone is described as beyond sins & virtues. Only a person beyond sins & virtues can liberate the individual soul from all sins. That is Lord Shiva alone. So that said, even the liberated souls like Veerabhadra & Kaala Bhaiarava who are Shiva Ganaas (devotees of Lord Shiva) are free from sins & virtues.

Valmiki Ramayan Aranya Khanda Chapter 63 Verses 4, 5:

पूर्वम् मया नूनम् अभीप्सितानि पापानि कर्माणि असत्कृत् कृतानि |
तत्र अयम् अद्य पतितो विपाको दुःखेन दुःखम् यद् अहम् विशामि ||

राज्य प्रणाशः स्व जनैः वियोगः पितुर् विनाशो जननी वियोगः |
सर्वानि मे लक्ष्मण शोक वेगम् आपूरयन्ति प्रविचिन्तितानि ||

Rama says to Lakshmana after losing Sita: I might have definitely, habitually and desirably committed wrong actions in my previous births and now I am reaping the result of all those impious deeds which is very much ripened and has fallen on me and I am getting misery after misery. I am deprived of my kingdom, departed from my own people, mainly Sita, my father departed and I am detached from my mother, and Lakshmana, when all these things are very deeply thought over they are replenishing the haste of my agony.

Here Rama himself admits that he is bound by sins because of the past misdeeds that he had done. There is a place in the Puranas where Vishnu takes the form of

Jalandhara and had pleasure with Vrinda and as a result of which Vrinda would curse Vishnu.

Padma Purana Uttara Khanda Chapter 15 Verses 42-44:

प्रियं गाढं समालिंग्य चुचुंब रतिलोलुपा
मोक्षादप्यधिकं सौख्यं वृंदा मोहनसंभवम्

मेने नारायणो देवो लक्ष्मीप्रेमरसाधिकम्
वृंदां वियोगजं दुःखं विनोदयति माधवे

तत्क्रीडाचारुविलसद्वापिका राजहंसके
तद्रूपभावात्कृष्णोऽसौ पद्मायां विगतस्पृहः

Vishnu (in the form of Jalandhara) after being fascinated by the beauty of Vrinda derived pleasure by uniting with her and he considered that pleasure derived from Vrinda as superior to salvation (SALVATION or MOKSHA is actually the highest peace that one can acquire from Lord Shiva alone), and he felt deriving greater delight from Vrinda than from Lakshmi. Vishnu after engaging in dalliance with Vrinda lost all his longing for Lakshmi.

This shows the power of attraction to the opposite sex. Even personalities like Vishnu, Brahma, Indra & sages are bound by lust. Vishnu couldn't control his desires after seeing Vrinda and forgets Lakshmi and engages in dalliance with Vrinda; on account of which he gets cursed by Vrinda. Except for Lord Shiva, everyone from the blade of grass to Vishnu are bound by lust. One has to surrender to Bhagavan Shiva to conquer lust.

Padma Purana Uttara Khanda Chapter 15 Verse 54:

अहं मोहं यथानीता त्वया माया तपस्विना
तथा तव वधूं माया तपस्वीकोऽपि नेष्यति

Vrinda curses Vishnu saying: "Since you came as an ascetic in disguise and deluded me; someone disguised as an ascetic will take away your wife in the future."

On account of the curse given by Vrinda to Vishnu; Ravana came in the form of a sage and took away Sita during Rama's absence and hence Rama makes a statement to Lakshmana in Valmiki Ramayana as we saw before, that he is reaping for the sins that he had done in the past. The Supreme Lord Shiva also graced Rama to defeat Ravana in the war.

Skanda Purana Brahma Khanda Setu Maahaatmyam Chapter 47 Verses 42, 43:

एवं रावणघातेन ब्रह्महत्यासमुद्भवः ।
समभूद्रामचंद्रस्य लोककांतस्य धीमतः ।।

तत्सहैतुकमाख्यातं भवतां ब्रह्मघातजम् ।
पापं यच्छांतये रामो लिंगं प्रातिष्ठिपत्स्वयम् ।।

By killing Ravana, Ramachandra had incurred the sin of Brahmahatya (slaughter of a Brahmana). It was to expiate this sin that Rama installed the Linga.

Shiva Maha Purana ShataRudra Samhita Chapter 22 Verse 46:

संमोहितः कामबाणैर्लेभे तत्रैव निर्वृतिम् ।।
ताभिश्च वरनारीभिः क्रीडमानो बभूव ह ।।

Fascinated by Cupid's arrows, Vishnu attained the highest pleasure in the nether world (Patala Loka). He began to indulge in sexual dalliance with the beautiful women over there.

This is another situation where Vishnu after attaining the nether worlds gets attracted to the beauty of women there and he indulges in dalliance with them and begets children falling into Shiva Maayaa. Mahadeva later appears as a bull to destroy the EGO of Vishnu.

Devi Bhagavatha Purana Canto 5 Chapter 1 Verse 32:

एकापि बन्धनविधौ युवती समर्था पुंसो यथा सुदृढलोहमयं तु दाम ।
किं नाम षोडशसहस्रशतार्धकाश्च तं स्वीकृतं शुकमिवातिनिबन्धयन्ति ॥

When a young woman though she is alone can bind a man down by the network of Maayaa like a strong iron chain, what wonder is there that the sixteen thousand and fifty women would make Krishna play in their hands like a Shuka bird and make him an instrument to serve any purpose that they liked.

Krishna was bound by the Maayaa Shakti of Parama Shiva & Para Shakti and he derived great pleasure by having dalliance with many women and surrendering himself to Cupid (Kaama).

So as stated before, everybody including Hari, Brahma, Indra & all the sages are bound by Cupid. The only person who has destroyed Cupid and has him under his control is Bhagavan Shiva. Cupid thinking of Bhagavan Shiva to be similar to other devatas like Hari, Brahma & Indra tried to induce lust in Bhagavan Shiva but finally, he was burnt into ashes by the fire that came from the third eye of Lord Shiva. That's why Lord Shiva is called Kaameshvara which means he is the Lord of Cupid or one who has Cupid under his control.

Matsya Purana Chapter 154 Verses 242, 245:

निरासे मदनस्थित्या योगमाया समावृतः।
सहकारतरौ दृष्ट्वा मृदुमारुत निर्धुतम् ।

स्तवकं मदनोरम्यं हर वक्षसि सत्वरम् ।।

Cupid (Kaama deva) bound by the Maayaa Shakti of Lord Shiva, taking his friend, the Spring Season, made an enchanting arrow of a cluster of sweet-smelling flowers over which the gentle breeze was blowing, then Cupid hit the chest of Lord Shiva.

Matsya Purana Chapter 154 Verses 250-252:

बभूव वदने नेत्रं तृतीयमनलाकुलम् ।
रुद्रस्य रौद्रवपुषो जगत्संहार भैरवम् ।।

तदन्तिकस्थे मदने व्यस्फारयत धूर्जटिः ।
तं नेत्रविस्फुलिङ्गेन क्रोशतान्नाकवासिनाम् ।।

गमितो भस्मसात्तूर्णं कन्दर्पः कामिदर्पकः ।
स तु तं भस्मसात् कृत्वा हरनेत्रोद्भवोऽनलः ।।

The third eye of Lord Shiva became ablaze as if it was going to consume the world and a terrific fire of wrath was produced. By the opening of that eye, sparks of fire began to fall in showers and Cupid was instantly burnt and reduced to ashes when the devatas cried out "Alas ! Alas ! What is this". The fire of the third eye then appeared terrible as if it would burn the three worlds.

Now some Shiva Dveshis (haters of Lord Shiva) inorder to denigrate Lord Shiva would say that Shiva was attracted to Mohini. The fools don't understand that the activities of Mahadeva are divine and no one can understand his activities. Firstly, Mohini is not Vishnu. It is Para Shakti herself appearing in the form of Mohini which is clearly explained in Brahmanda Purana.

Brahmanda Purana Lalitha Maahaatmyam Uttara Bhaga Chapter 10 Verse 4:

etasmin anantare vishnuh sarvalokaikarakshakah
samyag ArAdhayAmAsa lalitAm svaikyarUpinIm

Vishnu worshipped and meditated on Para Shakti (or) Lalitha Tripurasundari the consort of Parama Shiva.

Para Shakti herself manifested in the Mohini form. Mahadeva united with Mohini who is none other than Para Shakti. Secondly, this happens for a divine cause. Mahishaasuraa was a demon who created great havoc for the devatas and Para Shakti manifested as Durga to kill him. After he was killed the sister of Mahishaasuraa named Mahishaasuri wanted to avenge the devatas for his brother's death. So she will ask an intelligent boon that only the son of Hari & Hara should be able to kill her. As we saw earlier, Mohini is none other than Para Shakti herself as Vishnu meditates on the goddess of the three worlds and she manifests herself as Mohini. Through their union, Shaastha was born. He would be the cause of Mahishaasuri's death. So Mahadeva's activities cannot be understood by anybody including devatas like Hari, Brahma & Indra.

That's why when Upamanyu enquires about Lord Shiva to his mother, Upamanyu's mother says to him:

Mahabharata Anushaasana Parva Chapter 14 Verse 134:

दुर्विज्ञेयो महादेवो दुराधारो दुरन्तकः।
दुराबाधश्च दुर्ग्राह्यो दुर्दृश्यो ह्यकृतात्मभिः।।

durvijnyeyo mahAdevo durAdhAro durantakaha
durAbAdhascha durgrAhyo durdrushyo hykrutAtmabhihi

Mahadeva is extremely difficult to be known by people of unclean souls. These men are incapable of bearing him in their hearts or even comprehending him. They cannot retain him in their minds. They can neither seize him nor can they obtain a sight of him.

So when the devatas themselves are bound by his Maayaa Shakti, what to speak of people who have hatred towards Lord Shiva and are always engaged in denigrating Bhagavan Shiva. They are eternally bound to take repeated births and suffer forever. So as stated before, it is only Mahadeva who has Cupid under his control. It is very important to overcome Cupid to make progress in spirituality and attain Bhagavan Shiva. So inorder to overcome and win over Cupid we have to surrender to that person who has Cupid under his control and whom even Cupid fears to go near. That is none other than Bhagavan Shiva. So one has to engage his or her senses in completely dedicating them to Bhagavan Shiva so that we are not affected by Cupid.

Mahadeva is described as the Lord of Gauri. We have seen many references from the Vedas, Upanishads, Puranas, etc. where Lord Shiva is described as the Lord of Uma, Lord of Ambika (umApati, ambikApati, etc.). The words Uma, Ambika, HaimAvati, Himavadgirikanyaka, Sri, Gauri, Annapurna, Aparna, Shakti, etc. very often come in the scriptures referring to mother Parvathi. The word Gauri comes in the Lalitha Sahasranaama (635th name). The divine Supreme Goddess Para Shakti is the giver of knowledge about Lord Shiva.

Sage Vishvaanara describes Lord Shiva as without clothes. We can understand this in two ways. One is that Mahadeva is called digambara → one who has the four quarters (north, east, south, west) as his garments.

RUDRAM Anuvaaka 2 (Krishna Yajur Veda Taittiriya Samhita 4th Canto 5th Chapter), Shukla Yajur Veda Vaajasaneyi Samhita 16.17: दिशां च पतये नमो

dishAm cha pataye namo

Glories to Lord Shiva who is the Lord of the four directions (north, east, south, west).

Padma Purana Paataala Khanda Chapter 114 (Dialogue between Lord Shiva and Rama) Verses 270, 271 (The same is present in Narada Purana Purva Bhaga Chapter 79 Verses 221, 222):

दिशोंऽबरे जटा केशा भसितं चांगरागकम्
महोक्षो वाहनं गोत्रं कुलं चाज्ञातमेव च
ज्ञायेते पितरौ नैव विरूपाक्षं तथा वपुः

Mother Parvathi says to Lord Shiva: The four quarters are your garments. Your matted locks of hair is your beautiful hair. You have the sacred ash applied on your body. The great bull is your vehicle. Your Gotra (lineage) and family are not known. Your parents are unknown. You have a third eye.

Here mother Parvathi talks about the unique features of Lord Shiva. His nature (TATTVA) can never be understood by anybody except for a pure devotee. Every devata decorate their body by wearing luxurious clothes and with nice smelling perfumes, etc. But Bhagavan Shiva has the four quarters (north, east, south, west) as his clothes and he has the sacred ash all over his body. Every devata including Hari, Brahma & Indra has a cause but Bhagavan Shiva's cause or lineage is not known. His parents are not known as he is SVAYAMBHU (INDEPENDENT). All devatas are described as having two eyes, but Lord Shiva alone has three eyes. That's why he is referred to as Trinetra, Trilochana, Tryambaka, Tryaksha, Trinayana in the Vedas, Upanishads, Puranas, etc. The form of Bhagavan Shiva itself is unique when compared to other devatas and meditating on his form alone, one will cross the repeated cycles of birth and death and not otherwise.

The second is Mahadeva's uniqueness is told where he is described as wearing the skin of animals as his garment after destroying their pride. Mahadeva is referred to as "KRITTIVAASA" in the Vedas. He is described in the Puranas as wearing the skin of an elephant as his garment (gajacharmAmbaradharA), the skin of a tiger as his garment (vyAgracharmAmbaradharA), the skin of a deer as his garment (dvIpacharmAmbaradharA) and skin of narasimha (man-lion) as his garment (nrusimhacharmAmbaradharA, nrusimhakrittivasana).

Shukla Yajur Veda Vaajasaneyi Samhita 16.51, RUDRAM Anuvaaka 10 (Krishna Yajur Veda Taittiriya Samhita 4th Canto 5th Chapter):

मीढुष्टम शिवतम शिवो नः सुमना भव ।
परमे व्रुक्ष आयुधं निधाय कृत्तिं वसान आचर पिनाकं विभ्रदागहि ॥

mIDhuShTama shivatama shivo naH sumanA bhava
parame vrukSha AyudhaM nidhAya kRittiM vasAna Achara pinAkaM vibhradAgahi

O Lord Shiva one who is the greatest among those who grant wishes and who is the Supreme auspicious personality. O Lord Shiva the doer of good, please be auspicious, beneficial and bear goodwill to us. Please place your weapons on the trees and come to us O Lord Shiva who is bearing the bow named Pinaka and wearing the skin of Narasimha (man-lion) as your garment.

Krishna Yajur Veda Taittiriya Samhita 1.8.6, Shukla Yajur Veda Vaajasaneyi Samhita 3.60-61:

त्र्यम्बकं यजामहे सुगन्धिं पुष्टिवर्धनम् । उर्वारुकमिव बन्धनान्मृत्योर्मुक्षीय माऽमृतात्
एषते रुद्र भाग स्तञ्जुषस्व तेनावसेन परो मूजवतोऽती ह्यवतत धन्वा पिनाकहस्तः कृत्तिवासाः

I make a sacrificial offering to Tryambaka (three-eyed Lord Shiva) who has a sweet fragrance, provides prosperity, health & wealth to the fullest to his dear devotees. Just like a ripe cucumber gets separated from the binding stalk, may I be liberated from death and get immortality (MOKSHA → liberation). Please accept this sacrificial offering O Rudra who is present in the mountain Mujavat with the Pinaka bow in your hand and wearing the skin of Narasimha (man-lion) as your garment (Lord Shiva wore the skin of Narasimha as his garment after destroying his pride).

SHARABESHVARA DESTROYING THE EGO OF NARASIMHA

So we see the word "KRITTIVAASA" or "KRITTIMVASAANA" comes in 2 places in the Krishna Yajur Veda Taittiriya Samhita. The supporting fact (or) Upa-Brihmanam is present in various Puranas.

Linga Purana Canto 1 Chapter 96 Verse 115, Shiva Purana ShataRudra Samhita Chapter 12 Verse 36:

नृसिंहकृत्तिवसनस्तदाप्रभृति शंकरः

nrusimhakrittivasanas tadAprabruthi shankaraha

Ever since that day (the day when Bhagavan Shiva appeared as Sharabheshvara and destroyed the pride of Narasimha), Shankara (Bhagavan Shiva) is said to be wearing the skin of Narasimha (man-lion) as his garment.

Finally, Sage Vishvaanara ends the octet by saying that everything is in relation to Lord Shiva. He is the inner soul of everybody including the aged, youth, child, etc.

Shvetashvatara Upanishad 4.3:

त्वं स्त्री त्वं पुमानसि त्वं कुमार उत वा कुमारी ।
त्वं जीर्णो दण्डेन वञ्चसि त्वं जातो भवसि विश्वतोमुखः ॥

tvaM strI tvaM pumAnasi tvaM kumAra uta vA kumArI
tvaM jIrNo daNDena vanchasi tvaM jAto bhavasi vishvatomukhaH

You are woman; You are man; You are youth and maiden too. You are the man with a staff; You are the one with faces turned in all directions.

RUDRAM glorifies Lord Shiva as:

नमो वृद्धाय च संवृद्ध्वने च (namo vriddhAya cha sam vridhvane cha)

Salutations to the ancient or aged one who is loudly praised by the scriptures and who has infinite fame.

अपगल्भाय च (apagalbhAya cha)

Salutations to him who is very young.

Mahadeva is the oldest of the oldest (jyeshthA) but he looks like a five-year-old kid in appearance. When Bejja Mahadevi considered herself the mother of Lord Shiva and engaged in Vaatsalya Bhaavam (motherly affection) to Lord Shiva, Lord Shiva was really bound by her devotion and appeared in front of her like a small kid to give her boons. Bejja Mahadevi asked for nothing from Lord Shiva, except for engaging in motherly love with him as a child. This is an example of a true devotee. A devotee doesn't ask for anything apart from engaging in eternal service to only Lord Shiva. Mahadeva replied to her saying that she has become the grandmother of the entire universe. Why so? As Parvati & Parameshvara are the parents of the entire universe and since Bejja Mahadevi through her unflinching parental love won the heart of Mahadeva, she acquired the status of being the father of Mahadeva who doesn't have parents and who doesn't have a cause. Hence Mahadeva addressed her as the grandmother of the entire universe. Mahadeva knowing the heart of Sage Vishvaanara & Shuchismati appeared in the Viresha Linga in Kaashi as a beautiful eight-year-old boy to grant boons to Sage Vishvaanara.

So however one wants to experience Mahadeva with love and affection, Lord Shiva fulfills those desires.

One point to be noted is that, in all the eight verses sung by Sage Vishvaanara, he uses the word prapadye, bhaje, etc. in every verse. He glorifies that there is nothing that is greater than Lord Shiva and he alone is the lord of all and then he says "I surrender to that Lord Shiva". Surrendering to the Supreme Lord is very important.

Surrender comes from having unflinching devotion. Unflinching devotion comes from having the intense desire (**abhilAsha**) to know about Lord Shiva. Intense desire to know about Lord Shiva comes by applying the sacred ash, singing the praises of Lord Shiva, hearing stories about Lord Shiva, etc. Hearing about Lord Shiva is developed only by spending time with devotees of Lord Shiva. In this age of Kali, we can find more people who have hatred towards Lord Shiva. It was foretold by Sages Dadhichi & Gautama. So a true Shiva Bhakta should be very careful about whom he or she is spending time with. If you spend time with a person who is engaging in Shiva Ninda (deriding Mahadeva), you will develop the same attitude. So one should have an association only with Shiva Bhaktas to progress in Shiva Bhakti which alone is the only path to liberation (MOKSHA). Association with Shiva Bhaktas happens only if one has done Shiva Bhakti in their previous lives and by the grace of Lord Shiva.

Kurma Purana Canto 1 Chapter 30 Verse 27, 28:

कुर्वान्ति चावताराणि ब्राह्मणानां कुलेषु वै ।
दधीचशापनिर्दग्धाः पुरा दक्षाध्वरे द्विजाः ।।

निन्दन्ति च महादेवं तमसाविष्टचेतसः ।
वृथा धर्मं चरिष्यन्ति कलौ तस्मिन् युगान्तिके ।।

Sage Vyasa says to Arjuna: Those Brahmanas who had been burnt completely in the fire of the curse of Sage Dadhichi formerly during the Daksha's sacrifice will be reborn in the families of Brahmanas. In the Kali Yuga, their minds are overwhelmed by Tamas (Ignorance) and they will censure Mahadeva. Theirs will be a futile pursuit of Dharma.

Kurma Purana Canto 1 Chapter 30 Verse 37-43:

अनायासेन सुमहत् पुण्यमाप्नोति मानवः ।
अनेकदोषदुष्टस्य कलेरेष महान् गुणः ।।

तस्मात् सर्वप्रयत्नेन प्राप्य माहेश्वरं युगम् ।
विशेषाद् ब्राह्मणो रुद्रमीशानं शरणं व्रजेत् ।।

ये नमन्ति विरूपाक्षमीशानं कृत्तिवाससम् ।
प्रसन्नचेतसो रुद्रं ते यान्ति परमं पदम् ।।

यथा रुद्रनमस्कारः सर्वकर्मफलो ध्रुवः ।
अन्यदेवनमस्कारान्न तत्फलमवाप्नुयात् ।।

एवंविधे कलियुगे दोषाणामेवशोधनम् ।
महादेवनमस्कारो ध्यानं दानमिति श्रुतिः ।।

तस्मादनीश्वरानन्यान् त्यक्त्वा देवं महेश्वरम् ।
समाश्रयेद् विरूपाक्षं यदीच्छेत् परमं पदम् ।।

नार्चयन्तीह ये रुद्रं शिवं त्रिदशवन्दितम् ।
तेषां दानं तपो यज्ञो वृथा जीवितमेव च ।।

Sage Vyasa says to Arjuna: Although the Kali age is defective in many respects, there is one great good point in it. People can derive very great merit without any great strain. Hence after reaching the Kali Yuga belonging to Maheshvara, a person by all means and with special care, seek refuge in Rudra, Ishana. Those who bow down to the three-eyed Ishana who is wearing the skin of Narasimha (man-lion) as his garment, shall become delighted in their minds and attain the highest spiritual world of Lord Shiva (Maha Kailasha). Just as the obeisance paid to Lord Shiva certainly yields all desired fruits, one shall not derive that benefit by making salutations to other deities. In Kali Yuga, the only means of purifying defects is the obeisance rendered to Mahadeva, meditating on him and spreading knowledge about Lord Shiva as told in the Shruti (Vedas). Hence, if one wishes to attain the highest region of Lord Shiva, one should eschew all the devatas (Vishnu, Brahma, Lakshmi, Indra, etc.) other than the Supreme Lord Shiva and resort to the three-eyed Maheshvara alone. Futile indeed is the very life, the charitable gifts, the penance and the performance of sacrifice of those people who do not worship Lord Shiva who is even saluted by the devatas (Vishnu, Brahma, Lakshmi, Indra, etc.).

Suta Samhita Yajna Vaibhava Khaanda Brahma Gita Chapter 2 Verses 35-40, 43:

वेदबाह्येषु मार्गेषु संस्कृता ये नराः सुराः ।
ते हि पाषण्डिनः साक्षात्तथा तैः सहवासिनः ॥

कलौ जगद्विधातारं शिवं सत्यादिलक्षणम् ।
नार्चयिष्यन्ति वेदेन पाषण्डोपहता जनाः ॥

वेदसिद्धं महादेवं साम्बं चन्द्रार्धशेखरम् ।
नार्चयिष्यन्ति वेदेन पाषण्डोपहता जनाः ॥

वेदोक्तेनैव मार्गेण भस्मनेव त्रिपुण्ड्रकम् ।
धूलनं नाचरिष्यन्ति पाषण्डोपहता जनाः ॥

रुद्राक्षधारणं भक्त्या वेदोक्तेनैवे वर्त्मना ।
न करिष्यन्ति मोहेन पाषण्डोपहता जनाः ॥

लिङ्गे दिने दिने देवं शिवरुद्रादिसंज्ञितम् ।
नार्चयिष्यन्ति वेदेन पाषण्डोपहता जनाः ॥

वेदबाह्येन मार्गेण पूजयन्ति जनार्दनम् ।
निन्दन्ति शङ्करं मोहात्पाषण्डोपहता जनाः ॥

vedabAhyeShu mArgeShu saMskRitA ye narAH surAH
te hi pAShaNDinaH sAkShAttathA taiH sahavAsinaH

kalau jagadvidhAtAraM shivaM satyAdilakShaNam
nArchayiShyanti vedena pAShaNDopahatA janAH

vedasiddhaM mahAdevaM sAmbaM chandrArdhashekharam
nArchayiShyanti vedena pAShaNDopahatA janAH

vedoktenaiva mArgeNa bhasmaneva tripuNDrakam
dhUlanaM nAchariShyanti pAShaNDopahatA janAH

RudraakshadhAraNaM bhaktyA vedoktenaive vartmanA
na kariShyanti mohena pAShaNDopahatA janAH

liNge dine dine devaM shivarudrAdisaMjnitam
nArchayiShyanti vedena pAShaNDopahatA janAH

vedabAhyena mArgeNa pUjayanti janArdanam
nindanti shaNkaraM mohAtpAShaNDopahatA janAH

People who follow false doctrines that are outside the Vedas are described as Paashandis. People who associate with those who follow false doctrines are also described as Paashandis. In the Age of Kali, due to the influence of those who follow false doctrines (Paashandis), people do not worship the ultimate cause of the universe Lord Shiva, the one who has divine qualities with Veda Mantras. People who do not worship Saamba Shiva, Mahadeva, the one who has the crescent moon on his forehead and who is described as the ultimate essence of the Vedas are described as Paashandis. People who do not apply Tripundra, Bhasma, Rudraaksha on their bodies are described as Paashandis. People who do not engage in Shiva Linga Puja and who do not meditate on Lord Shiva are described as Paashandis. People who worship Vishnu and engage in insulting Mahadeva are described as Paashandis.

In the above references from Suta Samhita & Kurma Purana, we can see how Shiva Ninda (deriding Mahadeva) will be spread in Kali Yuga. So people who associate with them are also described as Paashandis as per Sage Suta. So one should always engage in spending time with Shiva Bhaktas, applying the

Tripundra, Bhasma, Rudraaksha, worshipping the Shiva Linga, meditating on the form of Bhagavan Shiva within the Shiva Linga and worshipping him alone by which one can transcend the repeated cycles of birth and death.

EPILOGUE

At the beginning of my book, I would have stated that the word "**abhilAsha**" means desire (or) wish. One should have that intense desire to know more about Bhagavan Shiva. Sage Vishvaanara had the desire to glorify Bhagavan Shiva. He sang this beautiful octet experiencing horripilation of joy after having the vision of Bhagavan Shiva as a beautiful eight-year-old child. In this world, we have an urge for different things: earning more money, fame, wealth, power, sex, etc. But whatever pleasure we go behind in this material world, that is temporary. It lasts only for a short span.

Narada Purana Uttara Bhaga Chapter 73: The Greatness of Tryambakeshvara: Verse 115:

क्रोशंतमीशं पतितं भवाब्धौ नाकुस्थमंडूकमिवातिभीतम् ।
कदा नु मां रक्षति देवदेवो हिरण्यरूपः स हिरण्यसंदृक् ।।

Sage Jaimini says: When will that Lord of the devatas, Bhagavan Shiva who has golden features and golden splendor protect me? I am shouting to the Supreme Lord. ***I am fallen into this ocean of worldly existence. I am very much frightened by this worldly existence which is like a frog stationed in an anthill wherein a serpent dwells.***

Sage Jaimini describes this ocean of worldly existence as dangerous and frightening. The more we try to derive pleasure in this world, the more we will end up in misery. So one should start utilizing everything in the service of Maheshvara as everything (sentient, non-sentient) belongs to him. Everlasting happiness can be granted only by Mahadeva. One should develop an intense desire to know and attain Lord Shiva. Once that happens, Lord Shiva himself directs the individual soul to take spiritual initiation from a Vaidika Shaiva GURU (who is a practiser of Paashupata (or) Atyaashrama vow as stated in the Kaivalya, Shvetashvatara, Atharvashiras Upanishads). By upholding Shiva Dharma all life, one attains everlasting peace by going to Maha Kailasha (the highest spiritual world) and engaging in eternal service to Maheshvara with no return to this ocean of worldly existence.

MERITS OF CHANTING THE ABHILAASHA ASHTAKAM AS TOLD BY LORD SHIVA TO SAGE VISHVAANARA:

अभिलाषाष्टकं पुण्यं स्तोत्रमेतत्त्वयेरितम् ।।
अब्दं त्रिकालपठनात्कामदं शिवसंनिधौ ।।

एतत्स्तोत्रस्य पठनं पुत्र पौत्र धनप्रदम् ।।
सर्वशांतिकरं चापि सर्वापत्परिनाशनम् ।।

स्वर्गापवर्ग संपत्तिकारकं नात्र संशयः ।।
प्रातरुत्थाय सुस्नातो लिंगमभ्यर्च्य शांभवम् ।।

वर्षं जपन्निदं स्तोत्रमपुत्रः पुत्रवान्भवेत् ।।
वैशाखे कार्तिके माघे विशेषनियमैर्युतः ।।

यः पठेत्स्नानसमये स लभेत्सकलं फलम् ।।

This prayer recited by you called "Abhilaasha Ashtaka" (octet) is meritorious. By reciting it in my presence or in my temple three times every day for a year, all desires will be obtained. The recitation of this prayer bestows sons, grandsons and wealth. It causes all peace and quells all calamities. There is no doubt that it is conducive to the attainment of heaven, liberation and wealth. The devotee should get up early in the morning and take his holy bath. Then he should worship the Linga. He should recite this prayer for a year. A man without sons will become a father. In the months of Vaishaaka, Kaarthika & Maagha, one should observe special vows and rites and recite this prayer at the time of bath. He shall get all benefits.

अभिलाषाष्टकमिदं न देयं यस्य कस्यचित् ।।
गोपनीयं प्रयत्नेन महावंध्याप्रसूतिकृत् ।।

स्त्रिया वा पुरुषेणापि नियमाल्लिंग संनिधौ ।।
अब्दं जप्तमिदं स्तोत्रं पुत्रदं नात्र संशयः ।।

This Abhilaasha Ashtakam (octet) should not be given to anyone and everyone. It should be strenuously kept a secret. It can cause even a chronically barren woman to deliver. Whether a woman or a man, the devotee should recite this for a year invariably in the presence of the Linga.

Here ends the commentary of Abhilaasha Ashtakam, an octet sung to Lord Shiva by Sage Vishvaanara. By reading this one will definitely come to the understanding that Lord Shiva is the only object of desire according to the scriptures.

This book has been written by Karthick with the blessings of the feet of Parama Shiva, Para Shakti & the devotees of Lord Shiva.

REFERENCES

VEDAS:

- Rig
- Sama
- Yajur

UPANISHADS:

- Isha
- Kena
- Atharvashiras
- Atharvashikha
- Kaivalya
- Shvetashvatara
- Jabala
- Bhasma Jabala
- Brihat Jabala
- Katha
- Mundaka
- Chandogya
- Brihadaranyaka
- Taittiriya
- Maha Narayana
- Yoga Tattva
- Pancha Brahma

PURANAS:

- Padma
- Brahmanda
- Vayu

- Kurma
- Narada
- Shiva
- Linga
- Brahma Vaivarta
- Varaha
- Skanda
- Devi Bhagavata
- Matsya
- Garuda
- Vamana

UPA-PURANAS:

- Parashara
- Saura

SMRITIS:

- Yoga Yajna Valkya

ITHIHAASAAS:

- Valmiki Ramayanam
- Mahabharata (Drona Parva, Anushaasana Parva, Ashwamedha Parva, Bhagavad Gita)

9 798886 678109

Printed by Libri Plureos GmbH in Hamburg,
Germany